PERSONALITY TRAITS IN PROFESSIONAL SERVICES MARKETING

PERSONALITY TRAITS IN PROFESSIONAL SERVICES MARKETING

James B. Weitzul

Q

Quorum Books

Westport, Connecticut • London

Library of Congress Cataloging-in-Publication Data

Weitzul, James B.
    Personality traits in professional services marketing / James B.
Weitzul.
      p. cm.
    Includes bibliographical references and index.
    ISBN 0–89930–877–5 (alk. paper)
      1. Professions—Marketing. 2. Personality and occupation.
    I. Title.
    HD8038.A1W46   1994
    650.1—dc20   93– 41818

British Library Cataloguing in Publication Data is available.

Library of Congress Catalog Card Number: 93– 41818
ISBN: 0–89930–877–5

First published in 1994

Quorum Books, 88 Post Road West, Westport, CT 06881
An imprint of Greenwood Publishing Group, Inc.

Printed in the United States of America

The paper used in this book complies with the
Permanent Paper Standard issued by the National
Information Standards Organization (Z39.48—1984).

10 9 8 7 6 5 4 3 2 1

To L. Douglas DeNike,
friend and teacher

CONTENTS

FIGURES

ACKNOWLEDGMENTS

Many people extended themselves to assist in the development of the ideas presented here. Hundreds of professional service personnel, marketing oriented and otherwise, completed questionnaires, allowed me to ask intrusive questions, and graciously provided candid answers. My heartfelt thanks to them, one and all. These processes defined the data-gathering stage of the research and were a critical first step. The ensuing analysis, interpretation, and reporting of the material were equally daunting. I received particular help with these later stages of the project from three people. Edward Garvey, who was trained in both philosophy and law, made a significant contribution in terms of helping to organize the material into logical sections. John Hamilton provided the type of keen insights and penetrating comments that only come from an experienced consultant. Joan Korn patiently analyzed the material for consistency and overall uniformity. I am indebted to each of these professionals for their contributions.

Once again the entire marketing, production, and administrative staff of Quorum Books made my task significantly easier. Eric Valentine encouraged me to "keep the faith" and finish the work. Jeanne Lesinski was instrumental in converting my occasionally convoluted syntax into readable English. Jude Grant performed an equally trying task in seeing the manuscript through to production. My thanks to each of these professionals as well. The finished product is significantly better due to their efforts.

INTRODUCTION

This book deals with the identification, definition, and description of the human traits and characteristics that lead to success in marketing and selling professional services. It is research based and provides recommendations that are the results of studying professional service personnel (successful and otherwise) in action.

The intended audience of this book is people who want to learn about the personalities of such people. This group may include professionals, general marketing/sales personnel, and anyone interested in the characteristics of professional people who are *also* successful in the marketing/sales function. Moreover, professionals are increasingly working in traditional organizations and yet functioning as if they were part of a professional service organization. They provide services to departments within an organization and internally allocate and invoice their time to those departments for their services. Since these internal services are charged to the department using them, they have to be "sold" to the department requesting them. Professionals who work in such departments and who are involved in marketing their services should also find the material useful.

Personality is one of those popular words that everyone thinks they understand but for which few people can readily provide a definition. The definition provided here is limited to the traits necessary to be successful in marketing professional services. Accordingly, it focuses on the necessary levels of technical knowledge, intelligence, and interpersonal traits that lead individuals to marketing/sales success in professional service firms.

Technical knowledge means acquiring the education, training and/or certification and licensing to function as a professional in the working world. Typically, this means a college degree with specific formal training in a range of certain courses or technical subjects. It frequently entails the completion of some professional apprenticeship leading to a professional designation, for example AIA, CPA, FSA, MD, Attorney-at-Law, and so on. It is also possible to obtain other types of certification in lesser-known professional fields, such as securities, insurance, employee benefits, financial planning, and real estate, to name a few. However, the research reported here focuses on the former type of "professional" person rather than the latter.

Intelligence is a much misunderstood word. True, in some sense it may not be adequately defined. Some culture groups generally perform differently than others on standard measures of it. However, it is still a useful concept and can be employed in part to define the professional person. Intelligence is defined here as reasoning and problem-solving ability. Often the ultimate measure of a professional service firm's value to a client is its ability to solve problems in ambiguous areas. This requires intellectual ability in three areas: numerical, verbal, and conceptual reasoning. People with superior reasoning abilities in these areas are able to analyze, understand, and define issues (and solutions) that people with lesser intellectual ability are not able to comprehend. So intellectual ability is a key aspect in identifying and developing more capable professional personnel.

The personality traits associated with success in marketing professional services are in some ways similar to the traits linked to success in many traditional sales positions. The traits include self-discipline, entrepreneurial drive, energy, and social dominance. However, it is the combination of these traits that distinguishes the marketing-oriented professional person from other sales personnel.

Marketing is an impressive and inclusive term. It includes the planning, organizing, and implementing of a successful sales campaign. The emphasis in this book is on the implementation of the sales campaign and the interpersonal traits that define people who are effective in the sales process. Planning and organizing are important aspects of the marketing process, but sales and sales credit are what distinguish the more successful professional service firms from the lesser-known firms. It is the ability to be face to face with a potential client and convince him or her that your firm is the one to hire for a particular assignment that distinguishes the best from the rest.

Identifying the right person to join a professional service firm is the first step in developing the person's market/sales ability. The enlistment, training, and development of the person are equally critical. Mistakes made along this path can deter an otherwise capable person from achieving success with the firm. However, it is the individual's personality or behavior style that influences his or her degree of success. Properly identifying and managing the person and recognizing that the individual demonstrates a particular personality type will greatly enhance the probability of the individual's success in the firm.

Professional service firms are defined here to mean primarily consulting organizations, and the individuals who populate them. The functions represented in this study include accounting, actuarial services, advertising, architectural design, compensation, communication, construction, employee benefits, engineering, financial planning, legal services, public relations, and recruiting, among others.

These firms are composed of professionals who provide very specialized services to more traditional organizations. Many of the professionals who work in such organizations are among the best in their fields. The "humor of joke," popularized by Robert Townsend in his book *Up the Organization*,[1] that somewhat sarcastically described a consultant as the person who borrowed your watch to tell you what time it is, has passed. Today, the advice of professional service personnel is taken quite seriously. Such personnel perform extensive analyses of problems, write detailed reports of their findings, and even assist in the implementation of their own recommendations. The transformation of the reputation of professional service firms has been so great that Tom Peters, in his new book *Liberation Management*, suggests that they represent a model for the organization of the future.

Chapter 1 focuses on the immediate task of defining the services that differentiate the marketing/sales functions within a professional service firm. Separating these functions is tied to six specific levels of managerial responsibility within the organization. The higher a person advances in the professional service firm, the greater are his marketing/sales responsibilities. The range of responsibilities varies from level one, the entry level of technical competence, to level six, the managerial leadership involved in being a partner or senior-executive officer of the firm. The key factor that separates the position functions at each level is the individual's ability to market increasingly esoteric products or services to ever-distant prospects and clients. The higher a professional person climbs in the marketing-oriented professional service organization, the more he is required to find "new" sales opportunities for his subordinates.

Chapter 2 addresses the issue of describing and defining the essential characteristics of the marketing-oriented professional person. The key characteristics are identified as knowledge, intelligence, and interpersonal skill. Knowledge relates to technical subject matter that the person possesses. The amount of knowledge required varies by the level at which the person enters the firm, but every person is required to show some level of understanding of the technical information. Knowledge can be measured in a variety of ways, including the completion of college courses or degrees, professional certifications or licenses, and a "technical" interview with the candidate.

Intelligence is a broad subject, but it should be measured as part of the selection process. It is generally acknowledged that most people in professional service firms possess a high degree of general intelligence. The actual level of reasoning ability required to be effective in the firm can be determined by gauging the reasoning levels of the successful people already in the firm. However, three types of intelligence (verbal, numerical, and conceptual) are identified, and the means to measure these abilities in candidates are discussed. Identifying the right set of interpersonal skills is considered the cornerstone of developing a successful group of marketing personnel. Moreover, the right set of personality traits (knowledge, intelligence, and temperament) will generally produce the most successful marketing-oriented professional service consultant.

Chapter 3 provides the research base for the book and defines a set of seven interpersonal skills. It details the research on these interpersonal skills, refers to previous research completed on groups of general sales personnel, and finally provides an analysis of the research on professional service marketing personnel. The trait patterns of successful marketing-oriented professional personnel from a variety of service sectors—the consulting disciplines of accounting, actuarial, architectural, communications, compensation, engineering, employee benefits, financial planning, and legal services—were included in the research. The trait patterns of more successful professional service marketing personnel are identified and reviewed.

Chapter 4 applies the idea of people gaining a better understanding of each other to the specific areas of selection and assessment. The purpose of this chapter is to encourage managers of the professional service firm to better understand the characteristics that identify marketing-oriented candidates. The process of hiring new people is divided into two parts: selection and assessment. Selection is the overall process of gathering candidates, and assessment is the focused review of individual candidates. The importance of assessing individuals in terms of four key interpersonal subtraits (risk taking, drive, stress tolerance, and adaptability) is discussed in relation to the seven behavior traits.

Chapter 5 advances the assessment of potential new employees and focuses on their enlistment into the firm. The emphasis in this chapter is on signing up those candidates who possess the characteristics of a successful marketing-oriented professional. This is a key step. Identifying the better people is important, but actually persuading them to join the firm is the critical step in building a team of professional service personnel. By focusing on the candidate's behavior style, the firm can position itself in the best possible light with the candidate.

Chapter 6 reviews the importance of properly training the new professional. Unfortunately, it is easy to forget exactly how "green" new professional employees can be. They are generally well educated and technically trained; however, they often lack the sense of social facility that comes with age and meaningful life experiences. To some degree, the training process is designed to smooth over any obvious gaps in their interpersonal style and initiate them into the corporate culture. While this chapter touches on some general parameters of training, its general focus is on the behavior styles of the individuals who join the firm and how those individuals perceive and adapt to the training programs. Part of the focus of the introductory training that the new professional person receives should be on identifying the person's behavior style and understanding how to best reach him as an individual. The new professional person has a responsibility to perform whatever professional duties are required of him in the firm. However, many new professional people need to understand and accept the immediate necessity of learning to market/sell professional services.

Chapter 7 provides a framework for evaluating the professional person's performance. The prime topics are the fairly standard areas of appraisal and compensation. Yet, the method used to review these areas is the different behavior styles of the individual. Some fundamentals of performance appraisal are presented and reviewed. The primary parts of this discussion are from the perspectives of the manager and the subordinate, and they are reviewed in terms of the different behavior styles. Professional people with different behavior styles will view, use, and interpret the performance appraisal process differently based on their own behavior style. Moreover, any discussion of "effective" performance appraisal should include an understanding of the human dynamics (behavior style) of the person presenting or receiving the appraisal.

The same approach is recommended for supervisor/subordinate discussion about compensation. This very important issue will be perceived differently by individuals with differing behavior styles. It is important for every person to recognize, understand and accept the inherent strengths and limitations of their style and that of the different individuals whose compensation they are reviewing. The value of differing compensation schemes is discussed for the behavior styles in terms of the three R's: recruitment, reward, and retention.

Chapter 8 looks at leadership in the professional service firm. It, too, is divided into two primary sections: managers and management. The first section on managers investigates how a person's behavior style will influence his or her potential effectiveness as a manager. Each behavior style possesses natural strengths and weaknesses that will enable one to more effectively interact with certain types of people and in particular situations. Being more self-aware will enable the managers to effectively use their inherent strengths to manage others. The second section on management provides direct insights and recommendations for managing the different behavior styles in two distinct situations: first, how to recognize when the professional person is frustrated in a work situation; second, some appropriate steps to motivate, inspire, and lead the person from any stress-related behavior to more productive behavior. The emphasis here is on a small part of the overall leadership process, but these are two critical aspects of making the professional person more effective within a marketing/sales environment.

Chapter 9, the conclusion, emphasizes the importance of understanding and using the seven behavior traits described in order to more effectively build a professional service organization. The chapter summarizes and integrates the material into an overall system for understanding, identifying, recruiting, and developing professional service marketing personnel. Identifying the right people is an important aspect of the process, but properly developing and leading these people also contributes to the success of marketing-oriented professional personnel.

NOTE

1. Robert Townsend, *Up the Organization* (New York: Knopf, 1970).

PERSONALITY TRAITS IN PROFESSIONAL SERVICES MARKETING

Chapter One

TASKS

Gaining an appreciation for the types of marketing tasks performed in a professional service organization is the base of the material in this book. Defining the different types of marketing tasks that the professional is required to perform is critical to understanding the marketing person. This task analysis is at the cornerstone of building a *marketing-oriented* professional service organization. At first glance, these statements may sound like a high school science teacher proclaiming that understanding atomic fusion is mostly a matter of comprehending the atom. It may be a bit obvious and overstated but, in reality, understanding the tasks that people must complete is at the core of building a successful professional service organization. One methodology to define these tasks is the subject of this chapter.

The definition of a marketing-oriented professional service person presented here begins with identifying the marketing tasks to be performed. Simultaneously, the *level* in the organization that is required to perform these tasks is identified. The SKAP (Skill, Knowledge, Ability, Personal characteristics) profiles of the individuals who perform the tasks will be discussed later. This is a simple definition of the tasks and identification of levels in the organization at which they should be performed.

The following figure provides an introduction to the types of tasks and level of responsibility associated with each task in a marketing-oriented professional services firm. The steps rise from a low of 1, labeled Technical Competence, to a high of six, labeled General Management.

Position Level and Individual Task Responsibility Scale

6 . . . . General Management
5 . . . . Market New Products to New Clients
4 . . . . Market Existing Products to New Clients
3 . . . . Market New Products to Existing Clients
2 . . . . Market Existing Products to Existing Clients
1 . . . . Technical Competence

No particular titles are assigned to any of the steps, but generic titles like

6 = Senior Executive/Partner
5 = Vice President
4 = Regional Manager
3 = Manager
2 = Senior Consultant
1 = Consultant

would probably be appropriate for the marketing/sales tasks that are included at each of the six steps. Clearly, each higher level represents an increase in sales/marketing responsibility. Using this configuration, the consultant has the lowest level of sales responsibility, and the senior executive has the highest level of sales accountability. The higher a person reaches in the marketing-oriented professional service organization, the greater the necessity for that person to demonstrate sales and marketing expertise. While these descriptions are not intended to belittle the other facets of the professional person's responsibilities, they focus primarily on marketing/sales duties as they exist in a professional firm.

STEP 1: TECHNICAL COMPETENCE

To have technical competence means that a person demonstrates the basic skills necessary to perform the technical job functions. These functions may include performing professional services in architecture, construction, software design, engineering, law, medicine, actuarial service, business consulting, financial services, or other areas of professional expertise. The level 1 position does not necessarily include any requirements for sales activity, but the person should possess the basic interpersonal skills necessary to effectively function in a professional office environment. Level 1 is the most basic level of acceptable ability to gain entrance into the firm.

This does not mean that the level 1 person is weak in non-technical areas. He must still meet whatever level of SKAP criteria is established for joining the organization. The candidate may still have to be highly intelligent, thoroughly knowledgeable, and socially interactive in the workplace. He is required to perform technically competent work assignments and interact socially with clients about task-related issues. Some level 1 professional service personnel are technically superb and consistently perform at a high technical level. Many peer consultants seek out their advice and readily endorse their findings. Clients often want these technical wizards on their projects because they have worked with them and welcome their technical input on projects.

These highly skilled technical people are not necessarily proactively marketing the firm's products and services. They readily demonstrate a variety of demeanors. Frequently they are unassuming, mild mannered, and team oriented and are willing to do whatever it takes to complete a job on time and within budget. Everybody likes them for their technical skill, strong work ethic, and general ability to get along in the workplace. As a rule, however, level 1 people do eagerly work with clients in the process of marketing additional products and services, even though the position description does not include any direct marketing/sales reponsibilities. It may be that only people with the *potential* to develop marketing skills and with specific levels of interpersonal skill are acceptable even at this level. The decision to include such a minimal level of interpersonal skill is part of defining the SKAP profile for an entry-level (technically competent) person.

STEP 2: MARKET EXISTING PRODUCTS TO EXISTING CLIENTS

A person designated to market existing products to existing clients is one who demonstrates the basic SKAP profile to perform functions at levels 1 and 2. Because level 2 is the first at which some marketing skills are required, the level 2 person must be technically competent and also able to market the firm's existing products to existing clients. This may seem like a small step up from level 1, but it can represent a significant increase in interpersonal skills. Some people have great technical expertise but have few marketing skills. The two skills though different are not mutually exclusive; yet, it is important to recognize that some people possess one skill while others are graced with both.

The SKAP profile of the person at level 2 reveals that he or she is technically competent but also possesses some marketing-oriented interpersonal skills. This marketing-oriented person is *potentially* more valuable than the person who is only technically competent. The ability to market existing products/services to existing clients is the first step in the marketing process. It involves: (1) understanding the firm's products, (2) recognizing client needs, and (3) possessing the interpersonal skills to help the client recognize the potential match. Different professionals demonstrate varying levels of comfort in performing these tasks, but the growth of the firm is dependent upon such ability.

STEP 3: MARKET NEW PRODUCTS TO EXISTING CLIENTS

The person who can market new products to existing clients possesses the basic SKAP profile to perform levels 1 through 3. He or she is technically competent, can sell existing products to existing clients, and finally has the ability to sell new products to existing clients. Again, this can seem like a small increment beyond level 2; yet, the measurable difference in skill between levels 2 and 3 is significant.

The reason for this difference is built into human nature: simply stated, most people resist change. They prefer the status quo. People are comfortable with existing conditions and are not necessarily eager to change their current circumstances. The word *new* means a change in their life, and for most people *new* means risk, possible loss, and a difference in established habits. Although this is not an easy barrier to overcome, it can be accomplished. At this step the process of change in marketing professional services is generally made in one of four ways.

The first way to accomplish this progression requires years of marketing experience. It is frequently based on the development of long-term client contact. In this case, professional service people have strong interpersonal ties with their existing clients, who will provide them with an eager audience for any new products they care to present. The level 3 person typically has a well-established (even entrenched) relationship with his clients, and they like him, trust his judgment, and believe his recommendations.

The professional may also have a close personal/professional friendship with a key senior level person. The result is that the work is performed in a professional manner but, more importantly, the marketing effort to establish the relationship is based more on the personal contact than the technical competence of the professional. The professional possesses full technical abilities, but his or her interpersonal skills are the key element in securing the assignment.

The second way of gaining this progression to level 3 is typically through years of proven technical competence. In this case, the professional providing the technical service is less interpersonally skilled, but he possesses technical competence on which the client comes to rely. In the client's eyes, the professional's recommendations become "bankable." For example, as is occasionally heard in professional services, "If Joe (the professional consultant) said it, you can bank on it." In this case, the professional service person has created an indelible mark of credibility with the client. The client is available to him because he has repeatedly proven to be effective with them. He provides a valuable service and introduces the client to products that are especially appropriate for them. Sometimes the client accepts this person's recommendations, and sometimes not, but the professional consistently provides up-to-date and important advice to the client.

These first two approaches for advancing to a level 3 marketing-oriented professional are frequently used when professionals in the firm market to their own clients. However other methods do exist. A third alternative uses either of the two methods described above but with an introduction to the client by another member of the firm. The client may be new to the individual professional service person, but the client is an existing client to the firm. This means that an introduction to the existing client is made by another professional service person in the firm. In this situation the level 3 person with sophisticated interpersonal skills is able to market the firm's products using his superior interpersonal skill. Likewise, the technical person is able to market to the existing client by impressing him with his technical expertise. The key element of the transaction is that the *introduction* to the existing client is made by another professional in the firm.

The fourth approach can require some product/service that is so technically advanced in terms of current product/service availability that a short description of it almost warrants an audience with a potential client. In this case, the product itself, despite the level of technical or interpersonal competence of the consultant, warrants an introduction. It may be a state-of-the-art product/service that has gained popular support among other clients, or it may be that it has been mandated by the government—for example, a new federal or state tax regulation, OSHA requirement, or employee benefit regulation. In any case, the product is in demand and requires a comparatively high degree of technical competence; hence the need for the services of a professional service organization. The interpersonal sales skills of the professional are secondary to the technical skills necessary to deliver the product. Client interaction and marketing skills are necessary, but the level of product technical complexity and overall demand are so great that access to clients is almost automatic. Some sales are sure to follow.

STEP 4: MARKET EXISTING PRODUCTS TO NEW CLIENTS

To market new products to new clients means that the professional person possesses the basic SKAP profile to perform levels 1 through 4. The level 4 person is technically competent, can sell existing and new products to existing clients, and has the ability to sell new products to existing clients. Although this can seem like a small increment from level 3, the measurable difference in the SKAP profile between levels 3 and 4 is significant. To be at level 3 requires the professional to generate *new sales*. Level 4 requires the professional to find *new customers*. To highlight the difference in degree of difficulty between these two steps, ask any group of professional people to do both: To increase their marketing activity by marketing new products to existing customers, and market existing products to new customers. See which activity they enjoy and complete more often. Determine the source of the most sales increases. Measure which area brings in the most business. Almost invariably the professional person will create more sales with existing customers than with new clients. By way of military analogy, when a new island objective has to be taken from a hostile force, members of the Marines are called in to "take" the island. The members of the Army are then brought in to "hold" the island. In essence, the primary difference in performing these sales duties lies in the interpersonal skills of the people performing them. The higher level requires greater interpersonal skills.

The key reason for the dramatic difference between levels 3 and 4 is that level 4 involves marketing to new clients. The first three steps focus on marketing to existing clients and are appropriately grouped as a *sales service* marketing function. Steps four and higher involve marketing to new customers and represent a *sales development*[1] marketing effort. This single change from steps three and below to steps four and above requires a significantly different SKAP profile. Developing client relationships and selling products and services to new clients are dramatically different from servicing existing ones.

The SKAP requirements for the first three steps are increasingly difficult. However, taken together, they generally involve a large "service" component. The marketing responsibilities in these first three steps focus on preserving and maintaining the current client(s). In essence, the marketing effort is largely reactive. The focus is on building the volume of business these clients provide by reinforcing the comfortable attitudes they already have about the professionals in the firm and the quality of services provided. The primary function of the service sale is to continue an already established professional relationship. The client's preferences, habits, and idiosyncrasies are relatively known and reasonably predictable.

The SKAP requirements for each of the steps four and higher are also increasingly difficult, and they assume skills in the first three levels are present. Functioning successfully at level 4 means meeting new clients and convincing them to use the firm's services. This means either changing the prospective client's attitude about a firm already employed, and portraying the new firm in a better light, or introducing a brand new service or product and convincing the possible client to begin using the service.

All of the steps at level 4 involve change for the client—which, as was already discussed, is inherently difficult. In this case, the professional person must bring about a conversion process. The purpose of this sales development activity is not so much a single sale of a given product or service, but the establishment of a new client. A single, new client relationship, once established, can lead to additional sales. The difficult part is establishing the client relationship.

STEP 5: MARKET NEW PRODUCTS TO NEW CLIENTS

To be able to market new products to new clients means that the professional person possesses the basic SKAP profile to perform steps 1 through 5. He or she is technically competent and is proficient at marketing the firm's products and services at all the lower steps. Marketing at level 5 of technical competence and interpersonal sophistication requires consummate knowledge, skill, and ability. In some ways, this person is required to possess the widely different skills described in step three. He or she must be highly competent technically and interpersonally.

To operate successfully at this level, initially the professional must identify the potential organizations that are worthwhile for contact. He must gain access to the executives in these organizations and meet them on a favorable basis. Once contact is made, the professional must demonstrate empathy for the client's problems *and* appear to be the source for solving them. The level 5 professional is required to understand the issues that are crucial to the client.

Once this relationship is established, the next step is to help the client to understand the need for change. The client needs to accept the professional's advice concerning a new product/service that he is offering. The professional may need to foster some seeds of discontent with the status quo and guide the prospective client to learn for himself the value of using the new services. Once the client shows a basic readiness to accept the new product or service, the professional must encourage the client to actually make the change. This is the most critical step. The service professional may have to patiently convince, motivate, and cautiously lead the potential client to the final step of authorizing the new process.

The level 5 professional will then need to reassure the client during the initial stages of implementation of the service. However, the best professionals at this level will gradually lead the client to develop professional relationships with others in the firm who are operating in a service mode (levels 1-3). This means that at the implementation stage the step 5 professional is off this specific assignment and is looking for yet another new client to begin the marketing process all over again. Generating new clients is a challenging process, but it distinguishes the level 5 marketing-oriented professional from the others at lower levels.

STEP 6: GENERAL MANAGEMENT

A person at level 6 possesses the basic SKAP profile to perform steps 1 through 6 . As the name implies, the person who qualifies for this SKAP profile is not only fully knowledgeable of the firm's areas of technical competence and marketing skills, but he or she also possesses a broad level of managerial expertise that involves overall strategic planning and long-term firm development.

The person who holds this position should be both highly technically competent and possess consummate marketing skills. It is impossible for the individuals at this level of the firm to be experts in all facets of the business and to be able to market all the firm's products; however, these individuals should have one core area of technical competence in which they are considered very knowledgeable. They need not be the best in the firm in a given area, but they should be considered very knowledgeable. They also need to demonstrate a broad ability to effectively market the firm's products and services at the highest levels.

This position is *not* an administrative one. It requires technical knowledge and interpersonal skills that can be used to form new strategic alliances with new clients or to develop associations that will lead to new products. These relationships/products are then handed off to personnel at a lower level in the organization to further develop these relationships.

The primary function of every person at each higher step in the organization is to provide sales opportunities for the people in lower positions. The requirements for the higher positions are increasingly difficult and the risks associated with success in these positions are ever greater. The responsibilities at level 6 of a professional service organization reinforce the notion that "it's lonely at the top." Moreover, the leaders of the most effective marketing-oriented professional service organizations recognize this ladder and use it to increase their market share and market penetration. The other managerial (non-sales) requirements for this position are generally beyond the scope of this chapter.

In summary, the Task Step Progression outlines the six steps necessary to be effective at each level of a marketing-oriented professional service organization. Identifying the tasks necessary to build an organization is the first issue and basis for this book. Thus far a series of definable marketing-oriented levels have been presented. A SKAP profile of individual candidates can now be compared against a series of job tasks and levels. The following portion of Figure 1.1 is the first step in this process. (This table will be enlarged later in the book.)

Figure 1.1
Identification of Candidate's Level in the Firm

PROFILE for: _____
Candidate for position level (circle one)   1   2   3   4   5   6

The next consideration should be the identification and definition of the traits that individuals must possess to perform these tasks. This is the subject of the next chapter.

NOTE

1. G. N. Kahn and A. Shuckman, "Specialize Your Salesmen!" *Harvard Business Review* 39, no. 1 (January–February 1961): 94–95.

Chapter Two

CHARACTERISTICS: KNOWLEDGE, INTELLIGENCE, AND INTERPERSONAL SKILLS

The previous chapter presented a methodology for categorizing and defining the types of tasks that people perform in a marketing-oriented professional service organization. The next step is to understand the people themselves. Understanding people, with all their unique habits and traits, is not an easy process, but it is essential to appreciate people as individuals in order to build a marketing-oriented service organization.

Ultimately, any professional service organization is defined by the perceived quality of the product or service that the organization delivers. It is a simple but unequivocal truth that the better the people, the higher the quality of the product/service. The skills, abilities, and personal characteristics of the people in the organization will influence the daily output and continuous success of the professional service company. In essence, people are the lifeblood of any professional service organization.

What makes for "better" people in a professional corporation? Answers to this question are about as common as successful professionals. However, the most focused and pithy answer may be that better professionals in service organizations are the most effective at reducing the anxiety levels of their clients. They enable the client to direct his energies to issues that he can resolve—with the confidence that the professional is working on issues that as a professional *he* is best suited to investigate. In this way the client can focus his energies on his tasks and the consultant concentrates his energies on his tasks. This idea of reducing anxiety is something of a broad generalization, but it does focus the discussion on the ultimate results that the professional delivers—problem solving.

Since the ability to problem solve is fundamentally an activity of people, it seems rational to begin with listing the professional's most critical abilities. The people composing a professional service organization are the basic building blocks that produce the products and deliver the services that the organization markets to sustain itself. An objective and thorough analysis of the people in the organization is at the base of measuring the potential of the organization's output.

The emphasis on phrases like "Total Quality Management" in the production areas of business in the 1990s suggests the importance of quality products in the manufacturing processes. In a professional service organization, the "product" (which oftentimes is a service) is a direct result of the people who produce and deliver it. Hence the emphasis on people quality.

The identification of potentially successful marketing-oriented professional personnel begins with a SKAP (Skill, Knowledge, Ability & Personal characteristics) profile of the position. As the meaning of the words in the SKAP acronym can be confusing, they will be briefly defined here. *Skill* is defined as behavior that is learnable. A certain skill can be improved with instruction. A person's skill to perform certain acts is generally thought to be developed and improved with practice and feedback over time. *Knowledge* is defined as information, concepts, theories, and facts that are acquired either innately or through some form of learning process. *Ability* is defined as an innate or learned proficiency to perform some function. *Personal characteristics* is defined as the demonstration of competent social interaction behaviors.

A generic SKAP profile of a marketing-oriented professional service person would certainly include the traits of technical knowledge, social competence, professional work experience, education, intelligence, and interpersonal autonomy with a team orientation. Essentially, this means the person should have an education, some work experience, a high degree of intelligence, and the right temperament.

People employed in a professional service organization can be defined and measured according to three basic factors: knowledge, intelligence, and interpersonal skills. This list is not exhaustive, and certainly other useful ways exist to describe individuals in professional service organizations. However, these three factors include a significant range of critical characteristics. These factors can be carefully measured and *combined* to effectively describe a given individual's potential contribution to an organization. The behavior resulting from the combination of the three factors can be as important as any individual factor.

The overall integration of a person's level of subject matter knowledge, intelligence, and temperament can be used to pragmatically define a professional person. A high degree of subject matter knowledge, when combined with defined areas of intelligence and an optimal temperament, make for a superb professional service person. But what about other combinations of other levels of the factors? For example, are people with average or modest levels of intelligence, but reasonable levels of knowledge and highly disciplined personalities, capable of being successful in a professional service organization? These issues will also be reviewed.

Levels of knowledge can be reviewed, investigated, and double-checked for accuracy. Finally, an individual's temperament can be categorized in terms of specific behavior traits. The next section examines each of these factors in detail.

KNOWLEDGE

The initial source of subject matter knowledge for many professionals is college, possibly including graduate school. The secondary source of professional knowledge is generally work experience. Both of these sources of knowledge will be analyzed to determine a reliable way of interpreting the value of each in evaluating a person for a position in a marketing-oriented professional firm.

EDUCATION

Once a person's formal education is completed, it is then frequently followed by some form of board certification or licensing exam, which can require an additional commitment of schoolwork and study. For example, most accountants at the CPA level graduate from college with degrees in business and then work two additional years as auditors for an established public accounting firm while studying for the CPA exam.

Similarly, many actuaries complete degrees in actuarial science, math, or a related field, and then complete a series of exams that lead to the FSA designation. Law school enables its graduates to partake of the task known as the bar exam. Architects generally complete a college degree but are only certified after completing their AIA designation. College graduates in engineering are allowed to use the professional designation of Professional Engineer (PE) after passing a licensing exam. Some designations are a minimum requirement to work professionally in the occupation. For example, a person who graduates from an accredited law school but who fails to pass the state bar exam cannot practice law in that state. Similarly, the person who completes a college degree in accounting cannot advertise himself as a Certified Public Accountant unless he completes the CPA requirements.

Other professional designations, some recognizing expertise in areas like insurance, real estate, computer programming, financial planning and consulting, do not have exact requirements for college degrees but mandate their own list of technical or educational requirements. Critical here is that a college education or a professional designation indicates that a person possesses some minimal level of knowledge in a specified area. The operative word here is *minimal*. Just knowing that a person possesses the education or designation required to perform a professional function may entitle him or her to be considered for the position.

Of their own volition some professional service organizations establish such minimal standards for new employees, while others are required by law to establish such standards. For example, in order for a person to advertise himself as a lawyer he must pass the bar exam in the state in which he or she intends to practice law. Many states now require that a person be licensed to sell life insurance and real estate, which generally requires study and passing an exam.

Other standards are more artificial and are established by the organization that is hiring people. Hiring only personnel who are CPAs or who have completed professional industry certifications when it is not required by the state may increase the likelihood of hiring a capable person, but this criterion can also cause a company to overlook otherwise well-qualified candidates. Professional certification, like intelligence, motivation, and work experience, is best considered as one part of the puzzle that composes the overall person. In general, if not required by state law, it is best not to set minimal standards for any one facet of a person's background. General guidelines are frequently appropriate, to be used as benchmarks and reference points, but firm minimal standards in one area of a person's background can cause the firm to overlook otherwise well-qualified people.

In evaluating recent college graduates for positions in a professional firm emphasis is often placed on performance in school. However, a number of studies have indicated that in general, school performance as measured by grade point average (GPA) has a very low correlation with actual career success. The authors of these studies frequently conclude that academic performance in school is correlated with the desire to do well in school but not with the ability to perform in the business world. In spite of this "scientific" evidence, many employers insist on only hiring students with higher than average grades. Grades *by themselves* do not indicate ability to perform well in the workplace. This is an example of the use of an artificial standard that can exclude very capable people from an organization.

In all fairness, high grades can be indicative of a person's overall orientation for success or failure, but it is not sufficient to focus exclusively on grades in school as criteria for hiring. The person with higher grades, whose background also includes more activities, like sports, clubs, student government, and an overall record of accomplishment, is probably a more likely candidate to succeed in a professional environment than the person without that overall pattern. Grades are one indication of how well a recent graduate is likely to perform on the job, but they are best used in conjunction with other evaluation criteria as well. Even then, they are only a guideline of how a person performed in the academic environment. Ideally, the person also has some work experience that can be reviewed and analyzed.

WORK EXPERIENCE

Evaluating a person's overall work experience is generally a two part process. Initially, a person is reviewed to determine if he or she has the generally appropriate work experience to perform the job functions. An applicant's work history can be analyzed by reviewing a resume and asking general questions during an interview. Questions can cover such work topics as:

1. Which tasks were liked best?
2. Which tasks were liked less well?
3. Specific accomplishments and how they were achieved; for example, if working on a "group" project, what were the candidate's specific responsibilities?
4. What was learned from the experience?
5. How were especially difficult problems faced or resolved?
6. Describe some challenges—how were they met?

These and other questions will provide some information about the person's general work habits and stated abilities. They also provide insight into his or her motivational pattern and interpersonal style.

The second part of the process involves determining a person's technical skill. Evaluating the quality of a person's technical work experience can be more difficult, especially when a candidate appears to be very positive for a position because grilling a positive candidate on technical matters may seem offensive to the candidate. This seems to be true because asking pointed, direct, and technical questions of a candidate who has summarized his successful experience can suggest that the explanation of his work background was not fully acceptable. Any such apprehensions on the part of the interviewer are generally invalid. In fact, most qualified candidates will eagerly elaborate on the steps they took to achieve their career successes. They will be especially candid in describing their most recent position. For example, when reviewing the work experiences of a candidate for a senior management position, a successful candidate may openly admit that he no longer performs the exacting functions of his technical subordinates, but he will eagerly explain how he manages his subordinates from a more macro level. The successful professional manager enjoys describing his methods to an appreciative audience—and he or she will do just that.

Similarly, when interviewing a successful professional services sales manager, the candidate should be open in explaining the background of his achievements. Generally speaking, better sales managers will readily recall their groups' sales accomplishments with specific numbers for the past several measuring periods. Moreover, they will readily supply company documents supporting their stated accomplishments. Sales managers who claim any of the following or make similar excuses for not providing the records probably never accomplished their stated sales achievements:

1. The company does not provide those records anymore.
2. My spouse lost them when we moved.
3. The dog ate them.
4. A fire destroyed them.

Professional service personnel directly involved in marketing or sales are very proud of their attained goals. Typically, they carry the numbers indicating their success in their head and they keep written proof of them in a safe location. They can readily cite examples of how, where, and when they overcame obstacles to win development awards or new client engagements.

Technically oriented professional service people should be included on the interviewing team. They are probably the best qualified interviewers when investigating a candidate's level of technical expertise in a given area. Again, the better qualified candidates, be they actuaries, accountants, architects, business consultants, computer programmers, engineers, financial service personnel, lawyers, physicians, or other professional personnel, generally welcome a meaningful technical discussion of their skill level. The questioning process itself indicates to the candidate the level of technical expertise already existing in the firm.

For some positions in a professional service firm, standard or customized tests can be created to better determine a candidate's level of ability. These tools can be used to provide additional screening information about a person's knowledge level or ability to perform certain tasks. These types of tests have been used with computer programmers, actuaries, engineers, and others who are fairly recent school graduates and whose level of expertise is difficult to determine in an interview. These tests are designed to provide an additional level of insight into the candidate's ability to complete certain job functions, and the better qualified candidates will see such tasks as an opportunity to demonstrate their level of ability.

One form of such testing is to request that the candidate bring some samples of his work to the interview. These can be reviewed as part of the interview and the candidate can explain what he did, how he did it, and any corrections he would make in his next assignment. In order to ensure that the material represents the candidate's own work, he can then be asked to perform a similar (but smaller scale) analysis, interpretation, or review of a hypothetical problem as part of the interview. This work-sample analysis will provide the interviewer with some evidence of how the candidate reacts under pressure and is an indication of the candidate's actual level of ability to perform the needed tasks.

In conclusion, it is imperative to fully and candidly evaluate a candidate's work experiences to ensure that he or she possesses the skills needed to perform the job functions. This process can require a fair amount of diplomacy, but it will ultimately lead to better selection of improved candidates. These criteria for evaluating both education and work experience are further discussed in James B. Weitzul's *Evaluating Interpersonal Skills in the Job Interview*.[1]

INTELLIGENCE

In many professional service organizations, intelligence is a quality that everyone is perceived to possess in abundance. It is assumed that every professional person is intelligent enough to make a solid contribution to the firm. However, some people are considered to be especially bright, insightful, or capable of making persuasive arguments that by their brilliance can sway others. Conversely, some people are considered "slower" than the rest of the group. These people, although they have other complementary traits that more than compensate for their lack of superior reasoning ability are considered less intellectually able than some others. Even in groups where everyone is considered to possess "superior" reasoning ability, some people are recognized as being at the top, middle, or bottom of that superior group.

With all other factors being equal (generally listed as subject matter knowledge and temperament), greater levels of intelligence are preferred to lower levels. In a professional service organization where the levels of an individual's abilities are directly related to the quality of the product, people with higher levels of reasoning ability can make greater contributions to the organization than those with lower levels of reasoning ability.

Intellectual ability is difficult to define. Volumes have been written on the specific meaning of intelligence, and it is not the purpose here to summarize or interpret the findings reported in those tomes. Rather, intelligence is simply defined here as the ability to analyze, interpret, and synthesize material as quickly as possible. It is best defined in terms of the faculty to understand and communicate using verbal, numerical, and conceptual abilities.

It is important to measure intelligence when a person is joining a firm because an individual's raw reasoning ability is not going to increase. Like a new sports car, the person will almost never think quicker or operate faster than he does when he starts his career with an organization. Additional experience and specialized training may improve the candidate's skill level in a certain area, but his or her potential to shine intellectually will be limited by his or her reasoning ability. A person's actual performance will also be influenced by his or her level of technical skill, personality traits, and a host of other factors—and these will be explored—but the ability to accept responsibility for new, different, and atypical issues within the context of the firm's expertise is largely determined by the individual's level of reasoning ability. If the person does not possess sufficient reasoning ability to perform beyond a certain level, this limitation should be addressed. Some candidates may be selected for specialized and limited functions. The intellectual parameters for these functions should be discussed and set. However, generally the greater the mental capacity the individual demonstrates, the greater his or her potential for growth with the organization.

One of the most reliable and valid ways to measure this definition of intelligence is the use of standardized tests. Such tests as the Wondelic, Raven, Stanford-Binet, and WAIS are useful in measuring one or all of these forms of intelligence. The tests can be administered by experienced test examiners. Their various distributors provide technical information on the statistical validity and reliability, scoring instructions, and general population norms for comparison purposes. Some standard objections exist to using such tests. Critics argue that in general intelligence slowly declines after age 35, or that some people in the population may have been disadvantaged in their upbringing and hence may perform on the test below their actual level of ability. A person can probably raise his or her level of performance on a given test with practice. However, raising a person's performance score is not the same as improving his ability to think. Partially for these and other reasons, the results of intelligence tests should be thought of as a reading on a thermometer. They provide a data point of information about a person's level of reasoning ability at a moment in time. Intelligence testing is not a perfect process, but it is one method to gauge a person's ability to deal with verbal, numerical, and conceptual issues. Below are three major areas of intelligence and the findings that can result from analyzing each one.

Verbal Reasoning. A measure of verbal reasoning is included to provide a measure of the person's level of spoken vocabulary, verbal comprehension, and reading ability. These skills are generally critical in a professional service organization for the ability to communicate using the English language is crucial to success in most positions. Everyday conversation is the most common means of exchanging ideas both in the office and in presenting recommendations to clients.

This measure is also partially used to validate a person's "stated background." For example, if a person indicates that he or she graduated from college with a degree in English and is a frequent reader of novels, biographies, and fiction, but scores poorly on the verbal intelligence questionnaire, then we may question the validity of the person's claims. Conversely, if a candidate readily admits that he has little interest in reading and indeed does poorly on this questionnaire, then it *may* suggest that he needs to read more in order to develop professionally. Reading more will not necessarily raise the person's verbal reasoning ability, but it should increase his vocabulary and communication skills.

Individuals whose area of professional expertise requires strong verbal skills (for example, professional sales personnel) can and usually do perform well on this factor of intelligence. However, simply because a person appears to be intelligent and performs well on this single test, he or she may not actually be "highly intelligent." A person who possesses significant (but primarily only) verbal skills can appear to be highly intelligent in general conversation—or during an interview—and score well on a test for this single factor, but that person may in reality be more limited in the other areas of intelligence, for the ability to speak glibly and with a certain amount of social polish is not necessarily indicative of overall reasoning ability. Further investigation may reveal that the person possesses an overall average amount of reasoning ability. This is especially true in Western culture, where a great emphasis is placed on verbal communication skills. Therefore, it is worthwhile to test for other reasoning abilities as well.

Numerical Reasoning. A measure of numerical reasoning is designed to give a definition of a person's ability to deal with patterns of numbers. Some level of numerical proficiency is important for most professional positions, but it is especially critical for positions in actuarial science, accounting, finance, computer programming, engineering, and architecture. Questionnaires are used to measure a person's overall ability to deal with numbers, regardless of the particular "number-crunching" skills required by the position. A person's performance on such a questionnaire is also used to verify something he or she may have indicated on other materials or in the interview itself. Again, individuals who indicate that they completed degrees in math or accounting are expected to perform well on these tests. Those candidates who make such claims, but who fail to achieve reasonable scores on the tests may be "suspect" in other areas of their stated accomplishments.

The brightest people in an employee group will score well on both the verbal and numerical reasoning tests. The ability to deal with numbers and words is an indication of a broader-based level of general intelligence. In some cases, particularly for positions requiring primarily quantitative skills, a high score on the numerical test and a low score on the verbal test may suggest that the person has a "knack" for numbers but a dislike for reading or issues involving verbal reasoning. Such people are frequently very capable of completing single quantitative tasks (entry-level programming, auditing, actuarial work, etc.), but have some difficulty performing in broader-based functions that require proposal/report writing, general correspondence, and interacting with others in an executive group.

Conceptual Reasoning. A measure of conceptual reasoning is designed to give an in-depth evaluation of a person's overall ability to deal with issues requiring analytical thought processes. Such questionnaires measure a person's ability to understand, analyze, and interpret abstract material. Generally speaking, this intelligence factor is the most comprehensive single measure of overall reasoning ability. Some tests in this area have been designed to overcome possible disadvantages in education or cultural biases. Such instruments as the Raven Progressive Matrices require people to complete patterns of symbols to determine intelligence. These types of tests do not require any knowledge of the English language or any special training or familiarity with mathematical concepts.

People who score well in this area possess the ability to understand, analyze, and interpret complex data that is presented to them for the first time. They are better equipped to handle issues that are novel, and although they may have limited experience with some issues, they do possess the ability to solve problems. People who score lower in this area have difficulty appreciating new technology or analyzing unfamiliar issues.

Interpreting the practical implications of the scores from the various intelligence tests can be either simple or complex. If a person scores high on all three areas of intelligence, then the interpretation of the person's raw reasoning ability is fairly straightforward. The person probably possesses a superior degree of intelligence. However, frequently a person will score high on one or two of the instruments and low on another. This situation requires greater interpretation and analysis.

A few examples will highlight the importance of defining the person's level of intelligence in the different areas and of integrating the data. Assume that person A is a recent college graduate with a major in accounting. He scores high on the verbal, numerical, and conceptual reasoning tests. He is highly intelligent in all areas tested and he is recommended (from an intellectual point of view) for the position.

Assume that person B also with a college degree in accounting completes the reasoning tests. He scores high (when compared to other college graduates) on a test of numerical ability. He scores average on a test of verbal reasoning and average on a conceptual reasoning test. Generally speaking, high numerical skills are associated with the skills necessary to be an effective entry-level auditor for an accounting firm. In fact, a high score might almost be considered essential. A score in the average range (for college graduates) of verbal reasoning is probably sufficient for an entry-level auditor. Realistically, verbal skills (beyond the average college graduate level) are generally not critical for performing auditing tasks well. Also, average (college graduate) conceptual reasoning skills are generally sufficient to perform such job functions adequately. However, what is the long-term employment horizon for such a person?

Again, person B possesses solid numerical skills but average verbal and conceptual skills. This means that his ability to absorb new knowledge is limited. His inherent ability to understand, analyze, and interpret complex data from an array of new sources is somewhat average. The level of responsibility he reaches in the organization will be in some ways limited by his intellectual abilities. However, his advancement will probably be more strongly influenced by the two other factors in his overall personality: subject matter knowledge and temperament.

Person B may specialize in a fairly limited area of the business and become an expert in a narrowly defined field. In this scenario he will concentrate his energies so strongly on a given topic that he becomes an "expert" in it. This specialized subject matter knowledge may enable him to prosper within a professional firm—in spite of his limited overall intelligence. Second, his advancement may be largely determined by his temperament. If he possesses the interpersonal skills to manage others, lead client projects, and effectively reduce client anxieties, then he can become a successful professional with the accounting firm. However, if he lacks these interpersonal skills or the opportunity to master some specialized area of the business, his professional career may quickly plateau at a defined level. In general, this means that he will be terminated from the firm, or he will simply resign when he realizes that he is not going to advance beyond a certain "middle" level in the organization.

A third example can further demonstrate the importance of intelligence testing. Person C—a college graduate and an entry-level professional person in a sales organization—scores very high on a verbal comprehension test and moderately well on numerical reasoning and conceptual questionnaires. The person performs his job duties well and is recognized as a valuable team member. Such a person can probably fulfill the role of sales person well; yet, a person in the vice president of sales position will generally need to score higher on all three areas of reasoning.

It is important to analyze and interpret the entire set of intelligence test scores that a person achieves, and not just the test scores individually. This total interpretation will influence the likely career path that the person develops within the organization. For example, a person with an average degree of reasoning ability can become a vice president of sales and marketing with a professional service organization—but he or she will probably develop an emphasis on sales rather than marketing. Moreover, it is likely that this emphasis will be much more directly oriented toward sales activity than in the areas of designing, planning, or organizing a market strategy.

The primary purpose of testing the intelligence of job candidates is to predict their level of reasoning ability. Intelligence is a critical skill and knowledge of a person's intelligence is important to predicting a person's potential contribution to the firm.

Conversely, it is not always necessary to measure intelligence with testing in the existing group of personnel within an organization. The primary purpose of the testing is to predict future behavior. If a person has already joined the firm, then his or her ability to reason will be monitored and evaluated by peers and working associates. Generally speaking, people in this group will have developed individual reputations for possessing certain levels of reasoning ability. Their professional peers and working associates will generally be able to gauge from their work the actual ability to comprehend and complete new and difficult assignments. However, when a person is being considered for a transfer to a new department or for a promotion to a higher position outside his or her immediate department, and where the individual's reasoning abilities are not known, then testing for intelligence and thereby predicting this part of behavior can be critical. Failing to do this would be similar to not checking references and not verifying (to the extent possible) the person's claims of education or technical competence. Some people have developed to an art form the process of inflating their accomplishments. These people interact with skill and social finesse that can impress the most experienced interviewers. Other candidates can be humble and even modest about stating their reasoning abilities. Both of these types of candidates (and all others) should be tested for raw reasoning ability. Testing for reasoning ability is the most objective way to ensure that a person possesses the intellectual skill to solve unfamiliar technical problems. Finally, it is possible for a person to have "a bad day" and perform poorly on the tests. At these times the candidate can be retested on a "reliable" alternative form of the original test. However, this is an infrequent occurrence.

What are the possible consequences of not testing a person's reasoning ability in a professional service organization? They can be considerable and may have a long-range impact on the effectiveness of the organization. It is difficult to pinpoint exactly what course a person's career will take based only on the fact that he or she possesses a low level of reasoning ability when compared with others in the organization. However, several patterns have been shown to emerge over time. These include:

1. *Repetitious Behavior.* The person's professional behavior relies heavily on what he has learned and how he has operated in the past. He does not adapt well to situations requiring flexibility, creativity, or original thinking. He is constantly forcing a square peg into a round hole. He lacks the ability to see the implications of his own limitations and forces old solutions onto new problems. Eventually clients become tired of his traditional, overly simplistic solutions and change companies.

2. *Poor Selection.* Frequently this person is intimidated by people who do possess more intelligence, and he refuses to hire "bright" people. He denies this is the reason, but a review of his hiring practices will show that he consistently selects people who are intellectually slower than those

selected by other managers. Moreover, he also tends to select for promotion those subordinates who are most like himself in this regard. They, too, lack the significant reasoning ability required to optimally serve clients.

3. *Turnover.* Better peple who are hired into his work section will sense that he lacks the ability to understand their ideas and they will either transfer to another department or, more likely, will resign from the firm. The people whose level of reasoning ability is superior to his will (a) soon sense the futility of trying to deal with him, (b) assume that management is aware of his limitations and that they are deliberately ignoring the impact he is having on others, and (c) conclude that the department function that he heads is not very important. As a result, these people will leave the firm.

4. *Study Groups.* Many meetings are important and practical. They bring together people with diverse backgrounds and result in valuable input for group decisions. However, the less intelligent person will commonly use them to gain access to the thinking abilities of others and to usurp the ideas discussed as his own. He can misuse the intent of the meeting to hide his own intellectual inadequacies and yet gain valuable information without contributing in kind to the group.

5. *Poor Decisions.* Perhaps the most fundamental mistake people with lower intelligence make is that they repeatedly make wrong decisions. Their vision for a given problem is frequently shortsighted, and they are not able to understand or incorporate information from sufficiently varied sources to make an informed decision. This is unfortunate because their errors will result in lost time, money, and business. For the most part, their work will have to be revised and performed again.

The best and the brightest individuals of the employee group will score high on all three of the verbal, numerical, and abstract tests. Such people are intellectually multitalented and can be considered candidates for top-level positions. It is not recommended that only the brightest people be hired for positions in the organization, however, for intelligence by itself is not sufficient to make a professional person successful. Interpersonal skills are also critical to success in a professional service organization.

INTERPERSONAL SKILLS

The necessity of good interpersonal skills is readily accepted and endorsed by most people, but the term is very broad and amorphous. Like intelligence, it is assumed that everyone in a marketing-oriented professional service organization possesses sufficient interpersonal skills to be effective with peers and clients. Some people will express the thought that "by definition, people must have solid interpersonal skills to be hired and promoted in our organization." This generally goes without saying. However, it also begs the question: Exactly what are good interpersonal skills? This is not an easy question to answer. Simply stated, good interpersonal skills involve three components: 1) The ability to deal with a more advanced or wider range of people and technical issues, 2) the skill to resolve problems in a shorter time frame, and thereby accept greater levels of stress, and 3) the temperament to work effectively in a more ambiguous environment.

The level of interpersonal skill required to perform under these conditions in a marketing-oriented professional service organization is slightly different than that which exists among professionals in more traditional organizations (traditional referring to, for example, government, academia, or charitable or corporate organizations). The reasons for this are subtle, but nevertheless valid. In a marketing-oriented professional service organization, the technical issues tend to be at the cutting edge. The average level of job pressure is higher than in more traditional organizations, and the corresponding time-frame demands more intense. Finally, the level of overall ambiguity is greater. Thus the level of interpersonal skills required to be successful in a professional service firm differs from that of a traditional organization.

In some ways, the differences between individuals in a professional service organization and people in more traditional professional employment roles can be compared to the members of the crew of a ship and the members of the crew of a submarine. The individuals on both vessels are well trained, thoroughly disciplined, and capable of performing the tasks required in their job functions. However, one group (submariners) operates in a more demanding environment—and needs greater interpersonal skills. In a professional service environment, the professional service people, like the members of a submarine crew, are required to interact under more "pressurized" conditions. The professional service person is required to deal with more intense pressure, less direct structure, and tighter time constraints.

In the marketing-oriented professional service organization, the personnel are required to accept the more strenuous conditions as a base line of performance. In addition, they are required to market and sell products with some level of expertise. This marketing orientation is an additional contribution to the rationale for the increased level of interpersonal skills required to be successful in a professional service organization.

Successful job performance for a professional person in any work environment requires self-discipline and high ethical standards. Successful performance in a marketing-oriented organization requires the additional skill of effectively marketing and selling the firm's products and services. In its simplest form, marketing professional services can be thought of as a process that begins and ends with people. People meet, discuss a commodity or product, agree on a medium of exchange, and complete the transaction. As this brief description of a sale implies, interpersonal skills are important to the marketing process. The more developed the interpersonal skills of the seller or buyer, the more likely that he or she will be able to influence the outcome of the transaction in a predetermined way.

The person with the greater degree of interpersonal skills will have opportunities to take advantage of the situation and make a better short-term deal for himself, use his interpersonal skills to establish a long-term and balanced relationship with his counterpart, and set aside his superior interpersonal skills and help the other person make a better deal for himself. Any one of these outcomes is possible in a sales transaction. In any case, the development of interpersonal skills is critical to the sales process. The person with the best developed interpersonal skills is likely to exert greater control over a marketing process.

The interpersonal skills necessary to be successful in a marketing/sales position are well established. Papers and books have been written about the importance of achievement motivation, empathy, and ego drive as three of the most often cited interpersonal skills necessary to be effective in sales. Defining the abstract traits necessary to be successful in sales is not strenuous. However, identifying the individuals who possess these skills and influencing these people to effectively use them to market professional services is the difficult task.

Identifying individuals who possess the interpersonal skills necessary to be successful in marketing professional services is partially dependent upon identifying a person's behavior style. An individual's behavior style is his or her fundamental way of viewing and interacting with others. A person's behavior style will influence the type of interpersonal skills that he naturally demonstrates. That is, certain types of interpersonal skills are a natural outgrowth of specific behavior styles. An individual's behavior style will influence the types of interpersonal skills that he or she effectively uses. A person with behavior style A will effectively demonstrate interpersonal skills A. Additionally, a person with behavior style B will most effectively demonstrate interpersonal skills B. Person A can certainly learn to use interpersonal skills B, but his most natural and (effective) skills are those associated with his own behavior style.

Some behavior styles are associated with people who see life as a challenging set of goals to be met head on and enjoyed through all the successes and setbacks. Others see life as a competitive event and are determined to prove their ability vis-à-vis someone else's finishing second. Another group of people see life as a chance to make friends and enjoy themselves through associations and emotional bonds. Alternatively, some people see life as a half-empty glass but will never reach its potential. All of these people are demonstrating certain behavior traits, which will be discussed in more detail in future chapters. These separate behavior traits are the building blocks that form an individual's behavior style. Initially, it is important to analyze and understand the traits separately. Once understood as unique traits, they can be joined in patterns to define a person's behavior style. Succeeding chapters build on this definition of behavior traits and behavior styles to demonstrate how certain behavior traits and styles are associated with success in developing a marketing-oriented professional service organization.

Figure 2.1
Typical Range of Scores for Technical Competence and Intelligence for Marketing-Oriented Personnel in Professional Service Organization

PROFILE for: _____

Candidate for position level (circle one)   1   2   3   4   5   6

FACTOR	RATING								
	LOW			MEDIUM			HIGH		
	1	2	3	4	5	6	7	8	9
Tech Comp A					░	░	░	░	░
Tech Comp B					░	░	░	░	░
Tech Comp C					░	░	░	░	░
Verbal R					░	░	░	░	░
Numerical R					░	░	░	░	░
Conceptual R					░	░	░	░	░
Interpersonal Skills					░	░	░	░	░

The concept of the SKAP profile has been used in this chapter to define a format for discussing critical individual factors. Using this format, three specific factors that should be measured in each candidate were identified and defined. Each of these factors contributes to the success of developing a marketing oriented firm. To summarize, the three factors, as found in Figure 2.1 are 1) knowledge, described as Technical Competence A, B and C; 2) Intelligence, described as Verbal R, Numerical R and Conceptual R; and 3) Interpersonal Skills. However, measuring these factors is only the first step in defining the marketing-oriented professional person. The measurements should then be summarized, reviewed, and compared to the degree of skill/ability required for the position. Figure 2.1, which is an extension of the graph presented in Chapter 1, is designed to assist in this process.

The specific areas of technical competence will vary from company to company and for different positions within the same company. The areas of technical competence that interest the company can be decided upon in advance, and individual interviewers within the firm with specific expertise in those technical areas can evaluate the candidates on their technical competence. Some people are high on one or two areas of technical competence, but few are high on all areas of technical competence. The areas of intelligence—verbal, numerical, and conceptual—are fairly standard and can be measured with readily available instruments. Again, some people are high on all areas of intelligence, while others are high on one or two areas. Those candidates who are in the middle range of technical skill and intelligence are probably limited in their ability to manage a wide range of functions in the firm.

NOTE

1. James B. Weitzul, *Evaluating Interpersonal Skills in the Job Interview: A Guide for Human Resource Professionals* (Westport, Conn.: Quorum Books, 1992).

Chapter Three

DEFINING INTERPERSONAL SKILLS

Defining the traits and types of people that are likely to be successful in a marketing-oriented role in a professional service organization requires an understanding of people in general. The method used here to understand people involves studying individuals in terms of behavior types. This typing process is not meant to limit or restrict the unique characteristics that define people as individuals. Quite the contrary, it is designed to focus on the communal trait patterns that people share with each other. Our research shows that when individuals possess specific behavior trait patterns or behavior styles, they are more likely to be successful in the marketing of professional services.

The seven behavior traits are

1. *Overachiever.* Stable, controlled, diligent, constructive, self-controlled, and restrained.
2. *Entrepreneur.* Money motivated, competitive, driven, ambitious, goal oriented, risk taking, clever, and perceptive.
3. *Active.* Happy, sociable, well meaning, alert, enthusiastic, team oriented, group conscious.
4. *Passive.* Sympathetic, empathic, apprehensive, occasionally anxious, inactive, and ambivalent.
5. *Aggressive.* Determined, tenacious, power seeking, suspicious, assertive, forceful, and contentious.
6. *Sensitized.* Reserved, introverted, withdrawn, secretive, perceptive, intuitive, analytical, and creative.

7. *Compulsive*. Precise, thorough, methodical, systematic, orderly, purposeful, task oriented, practical, and logical.

Understanding these seven traits is at the cornerstone of utilizing the system described in this text. Gaining a familiarity with the seven traits will improve the selection of marketing-oriented professional service personnel.

At first glance, the seven traits introduced here can appear to resemble a short laundry list of traits that are used to describe a standard variety of behaviors. True enough, the list is short and appears relatively similar to any number of such trait lists. The unique aspect of this list, however, is that it was constructed to describe a vast array of interpersonal behavior *and* the longitudinal research methods that were employed to construct and validate it.[1] A brief overview of the origin, design, and validation of the seven traits is included here.

The seven traits listed here started as a longer list of traits. This shorter list was selected by a group of professional psychologists. The initial traits were thought to represent a list of relatively new and unique traits not explicitly represented in the professional psychological literature and was considered to be descriptive of a large portion of human behavior. However, additional empirical research to define the traits ultimately reduced the list to the present seven traits.

This research was conducted by selecting large numbers of people whose life histories and everyday manner manifested a series of behaviors that were consistent with the trait definitions. For example, individuals defined as having a high score on the overachiever trait demonstrated in their life patterns and everyday behaviors evidence of self-discipline, control, and a perpetual habit of overcoming significant obstacles—for the apparent reason that obstacles *should be overcome*.

Some of the individuals in this overachiever trait group were "hardship cases," who completed college degrees while working almost full time. Once in the work force, these individuals went on to attain significant career positions at an early age. These people simply accepted whatever handicaps they were dealt and overcame obstacles to achieve significant goals. They consistently showed a history of resolving problems, overcoming obstacles, and eliminating frustrations. They were determined to achieve specific goals and objectives, but they were less concerned with any direct or tangible reward, while being driven to reach whatever plateau of success they deemed appropriate. Members of the overachiever trait group consistently focused on achieving more than they had previously. At the same time, their primary motivation was simply achievement per se. The individuals were not necessarily highly motivated by money, status, or power. They simply were driven to achieve because it was the "right thing to do." Other people with less disciplined life histories were selected and studied in order to understand the people with average and low amounts of the overachiever trait.

This same method was used to identify individuals whose life histories reflected different levels (high, medium, and low) of each of the seven traits, and these individuals were studied and analyzed. Additionally, individuals were identified and studied whose life histories emphasized combinations of traits. The life histories that reflected a clear combination of traits were described as behavior types.

The end product of years of research on these behavior traits and types was a series of questionnaires that can be used to identify and categorize individuals. Individuals with known behavior patterns (for example, the overachievers) responded to the questionnaires in a manner that is statistically different from people with other known behavior patterns (for example, the entrepreneurs). In this way, the scoring of questionnaires of people who are relatively unknown provides a series of ratings on each of the seven behavior traits that can be compared to the scores of people who are known.

The most useful application of this type of behavior research is to compare the trait patterns of people in certain job functions with applicants for positions in those job functions. If it can be shown that performance in some job positions is enhanced by the demonstration of certain behavior traits, then recruiting applicants with those trait patterns would benefit both the job candidates and the employer.

For example, if a group of successful sales personnel were shown to have certain trait patterns, and another group of unsuccessful sales personnel were shown to have another trait pattern, a company might use the comparison as part of a selection process for new sales personnel. If the company wanted to hire potentially more successful sales personnel, then the company might consider basing part of the selection process for sales personnel on an evaluation of the candidates' trait patterns.

A study was conducted to do just that. It analyzed over 3,000 candidates for sales positions and compared their trait patterns to the known trait patterns of successful sales personnel. The conclusion of this three-year longitudinal study was that the questionnaires were highly successful in selecting new candidates to be successful in sales positions.[2]

The research study reported in Weitzul's *Evaluating Interpersonal Skills in the Job Interview* followed similar procedures as the study of the 3,000 sales candidates. The current study measured and categorized the behavior trait patterns of hundreds of marketing-oriented personnel in professional service firms. Each person was a professional who as part of his job description was engaged in the marketing and sales of professional services. The individuals were not primarily sales personnel within a consulting firm, but were professional members of the firm who had demonstrated the skills to be successful in the marketing and sales areas. The professionals in this group were considered the "experimental" group.

Each person was rated by the management of his or her firm as being "marketing/sales oriented" and having achieved a high degree of success in marketing the firm's products and services. A cross-section of professional firms participated in the study, including accounting, actuarial science, architecture, communications, compensation, engineering, employee benefits, financial planning, and legal services. This diversity of professional service consulting personnel was deliberate. The purpose of the study was to determine the value of the material for marketing-oriented professional service personnel, not exclusively consultants in a particular industry.

Two ratings for each person were computed. The first rating was based on the Position Level and Individual Task Responsibility Scale, as described in Chapter 1. This rating was designed to measure a person's level of marketing task/responsibility in a professional service organization. The ratings ranged from 1 (Technical Competence) to 6 (General Management). They are repeated here:

Position Level and Individual Task Responsibility Scale

6 . . . . General Management
5 . . . . Market New Products to New Clients
4 . . . . Market Existing Products to New Clients
3 . . . . Market New Products to Existing Clients
2 . . . . Market Existing Products to Existing Clients
1 . . . . Technical Competence

These six levels are intended to demarcate specific differences of marketing/sales task responsibility in a professional service firm. No particular titles are assigned to any of the steps, but generic titles like 6 = Senior Executive/Partner, 5 = Vice-President, 4 = Regional Manager, 3 = Manager, 2 = Senior Consultant, 1 = Consultant may be appropriate. However, it should be remembered that the selection criteria for placing a person into one of the six levels is not the title (consultant, regional manager, vice-president, etc.), but only the marketing/sales job function.

The second rating was the person's score on each of the seven traits. These same individuals (who were rated between 1 and 6 on the Position Level Scale) completed a series of questionnaires and were rated on each of the seven behavior traits. These ratings ranged from 1, indicating a very low amount of the trait (in the bottom 10 percent of people completing the questionnaires), to 9, indicating a very high amount of the trait (in the top 90 percent of the people completing the questionnaires). The results of these ratings are presented here.

Figure 3.1 indicates the range of scores for all the professional personnel who completed the questionnaires, while Figure 3.2 indicates the *average behavior trait score* for the Position Level and Individual Task Responsibility Scale. The numerical score rankings of 1 to 9, and the qualitative rankings of high, medium, and low, are determined statistically. The 1 to 9 rankings represent stanines from 10 to 99, with 1 representing the percentages 10 to 19, 2 representing the percentages 20 to 29, and so on. They are based on the range of responses of the professional service marketing personnel who completed a series of behavior trait questionnaires. The figure indicates that when all the professional personnel in this study are considered, the scores on the over-

Figure 3.1
Range of Behavior Trait Scores for Marketing-Oriented Professional Service Personnel

SEVEN TRAITS	CATEGORY								
	LOW			MEDIUM			HIGH		
	1	2	3	4	5	6	7	8	9
Overachiever							░	░	░
Entrepreneur					░	░	░	░	
Active					░	░	░	░	
Passive		░	░	░	░	░			
Sensitized		░	░	░	░	░			
Aggressive						░	░	░	░
Compulsive				░	░	░			

Figure 3.2
Average Behavior Trait Scores for the Position Level and Individual Task Responsibility Scale

SEVEN TRAITS	CATEGORY								
	LOW			MEDIUM			HIGH		
	1	2	3	4	5	6	7	8	9
Overachiever					A	B	C	D	
Entrepreneur				A	B		D	C	
Active				A	B	C		D	
Passive			C	B	A D				
Sensitized			C	B	D A				
Aggressive				A	B		C	D	
Compulsive				A	B C		D		

achiever trait ranged from approximately 60 percent to 95 percent of all people who completed the questionnaires.

These scores can be used as a starting point to rank candidates in terms of the traits. Using this figure as a guide, the most successful marketing-oriented personnel (on average) will score in the high range on the overachiever, entrepreneur, active, and aggressive traits. They will score in the low range on the passive and sensitized traits. Finally, they will score in the middle range on the compulsive trait.

The next step of the process was to compare the individual professional marketing personnel ratings for the Position Level and Individual Task Responsibility Scale with the score on *each* of the seven behavior traits (overachiever, entrepreneur, active, passive, sensitized, aggressive, compulsive). These results are presented in Figure 3.2.

Some of the sample sizes (the number of people at each level who completed the behavior trait questionnaires) were relatively small. Therefore, some of the position level categories were combined for statistical purposes. This resulted in the six position levels being reduced to four position levels. The newly formed position levels were composed as follows:

Group A Levels 1 and 2 combined (Technical Competence and Market Existing Products to Existing Clients)

Group B Level 3 (Market New Products to Existing Clients)

Group C Level 4 (Market Existing Products to New Clients)

Group D Levels 5 and 6 combined (Market New Products to New Clients and General Management)

In general, Group A is composed of the people with the lowest level of marketing responsibilities. Conversely, Group D is composed of the people with the highest level of marketing responsibilities. At first glance the information in Figure 3.2 may appear confusing. However, once the labels are understood, the figure is actually quite rich in meaningful information. The seven behavior traits are listed in the far left column. Once again, the numerical score rankings of 1 to 9, and the qualitative rankings of high, medium, and low are determined statistically. The 1 to 9 rankings represent stanines from 10 to 99, with 1 representing the percentages 10 to 19, 2 representing the percentages 20 to 29, and so on. They are based on the range of responses of the professional service marketing personnel who completed a series of behavior trait questionnaires.

The letters A, B, C, and D refer to the group levels previously defined above. Each letter (A, B, C, and D) in each behavior trait row (overachiever, entrepreneur, active, etc.) represents the average percentage of the individuals in that group for that behavior trait. For example, in reviewing the overachiever trait, the following percentages are represented:

1. The average percent ranking of the A group was 52.

2. The average percent ranking of the B group was 60.

3. The average percent ranking of the C group was 76.

4. The average percent ranking of the D group was 82.

Some general interpretation of Figure 3.2 is necessary. For the most part, the higher the level of marketing responsibility, the higher the scores on the overachiever, entrepreneur, active, and aggressive traits. It is *almost* consistent that the order of the groups—which defines level of responsibility—is associated with the scores on the traits. Group A, with the lowest level of marketing responsibilities, is lowest on the overachiever, entrepreneur, active, and aggressive traits, whereas Group D, with the highest level of marketing responsibilities, is highest on the overachiever, active, and aggressive traits, and second highest on the entrepreneur trait.

However, it is unlikely that every worthy candidate will score exactly the same as in this figure. In fact, few will. Almost all superior professional marketing people will score in the high range of the overachiever. These people possess discipline, honesty, emotional control, and a strong sense of task accomplishment. They will also score in the high range on one or two of the entrepreneur, active, and aggressive traits. It is very unlikely that they will score high in all four of these traits. This means that the typically successful marketing-oriented professional person is high on the overachiever and some combination of the entrepreneur, active, and aggressive categories. At the same time, he or she will score low on the passive and sensitized traits, and most frequently, in the middle range for the compulsive trait.

Again, exceptions to the general rule can exist. The most common example is the person who scores high on the overachiever, active, and passive traits. So Figure 3.2 should be used as a guide, not an absolute rule in making decisions concerning the selection of new marketing-oriented professional personnel.

It is also true that the higher-level positions are filled with people who possess more maturity, experience, and skill. However, the measurement of the traits is *independent* of these factors. Previous research has shown that a person's trait pattern is formed by about the chronological age of 20 years, and it remains generally constant throughout life. So the higher scores on the behavior traits for marketing personnel with broader responsibilities reflect the relatively constant behavior trait patterns of those individuals. The behavior trait patterns were not "learned" on the job but were formed by the time of early adulthood and maintained by the individuals into their current positions. The ability to perform the marketing functions required may (have been) improved by training, but the trait patterns remained constant.

One other general observation is that the Group C individuals scored (on average) highest of any group in the entrepreneur trait and lower than any other group on the passive and sensitized traits. This *suggests* that the Group C individuals are more individually motivated, competitive, driven, and ambitious than their counterparts in either groups A, B, or D. While it may have been expected that the members of Group C would show more of these traits than the members of the A or B groups, it is somewhat surprising that they are so different from members of Group D.

Again, the data *suggest* that while the behaviors of competitive, individualistic drive will advance a person to Group C of marketing responsibilities, the advancement to Group D requires a softer, more group-oriented (high overachiever, active, or aggressive traits) approach than the typically successful Group C person demonstrates. This idea is reinforced by the data when it is noted that the Group D individuals also score relatively high on the passive and sensitized traits.

A "control" group of professional service personnel was also studied. This control group consisted of approximately 200 professional personnel in the same firms and operating at the same levels as the professionals in the experimental group. The only major difference between members of the two groups is that the professionals in the control group were *not* considered as successful in marketing the firms' products and services as the members of the experimental group. The professionals in the control group scored differently from their counterparts in the experimental groups on the behavior traits. Their scores on trait patterns indicated that they possessed different behavior styles from the experimental group (successful marketing professionals at each of the six position levels). The details of these differences are available from the author.

NOTES

1. A full account of the development of the traits is available from the author: James B. Weitzul, Banks & Weitzul, P.O. Box 2351, 2 Research Way, Princeton, NJ 08540.

2. The use of these questionnaires in selecting personnel for a variety of positions is more fully explained in James B. Weitzul, *Evaluating Interpersonal Skills in the Job Interview: A Guide for Human Resource Professionals* (Westport, Conn.: Quorum Books, 1992).

Chapter Four

RECRUITMENT: SELECTION AND ASSESSMENT

Recruiting new professionals for a marketing-oriented professional service organization is serious business. Asking existing members of the firm to spend time on recruiting when they could be performing more revenue-generating tasks is a significant request. However, the alternative of allowing some well-meaning but not totally informed person to complete this task is generally a recipe for long-term disaster. This is true because in the absence of input from senior people in the firm, and a defined set of guidelines or SKAP profile of what the candidate's skill profile should include, the person performing the recruiting function is largely operating in a vacuum. Without the involvement of senior personnel and a definite SKAP profile of criteria, the quality of applicants to join the firm may subtly but consistently decline. Unfortunately, as the quality of the applicant pool declines, so does the quality of the candidates who are hired. Eventually, the overall value of the products and services that the professional service organization provides will also fall off, and the firm itself will lose its credibility and will self-destruct.

The recruitment process requires attention to three key variables: selection, assessment, and enlistment. Selection and assessment will be discussed in this chapter. Enlistment, which is the process of persuading the selected and assessed candidates to join the firm, will be discussed in the next chapter. Each of these variables is equally important in the process of bringing people into the organization. Focusing on these factors to recruit people effectively allows the company to concentrate its resources on the better candidates. This is important because recruiting is an expensive and time-consuming process.

Selecting a pool of candidates who demonstrate the traits to be successful is the first step. This means inviting a range of candidates to be interviewed and evaluated by members of the firm. Assessing the individual candidates is the next step. The more effective the selection process, the easier the assessment process, for the two steps are designed to work together. Assessment is the continuation of selection. If selection is thought of as a rough sorting of applicants, assessment should be considered the fine sorting. The difference is obviously one of degree, and generally the assessment process is going to be a finer, more careful analysis of the candidates interviewing for the position.

SELECTION

The development of a group of disciplined, focused, and effective professional service personnel is founded on a solid program of selection. In the ultimate analysis, the better the candidate pool, the more effective the resultant members of the organization will be. Many dollars are spent every year in order to absolutely guarantee methods for organizations to find capable marketing-oriented professional personnel. The usage of most of these methods represents false hopes and leads to additional frustration for the organization. There are no short cuts, quick fixes, or easy ways to locate and select disciplined and energetic marketing-oriented professional personnel. The successful completion of the process requires time.

The ideal time to save money in the recruiting process is at the selection stage. If appropriate candidates are selected and enlisted, then a considerable amount of money will be saved. Conversely, if inappropriate candidates are selected and enlisted, then significant amounts of money will be wasted. The primary cause of this expense is turnover. However, the lost costs in terms of training, client exposure, marketing opportunities, and rehire must be added to the single category of turnover. The optimum time for reducing these costs is before the professional person is hired. If the wrong people are selected for a marketing-oriented firm, then almost no amount of training, incentive compensation, performance appraisal, and motivational leadership will improve them. Simply stated, the key to reducing professional service marketing person turnover is to recruit capable people. The financial impact of an *in*effective recruiting program is well documented. The turnover figures for the people offering professional services (consulting) are high, and the costs of that turnover have been calculated by as many people as offer solutions to the problem.

The most common and expensive problem associated with poor selection is the acceptance of the classic "just-good-enough" professional person. This is the professional person who performs well enough to maintain his position on the team but barely well enough to ever qualify for consideration for the next higher level. He or she is generally considered to be good enough to keep but not bad enough to go through the process of firing. Such people seldom leave a position of their own accord. Their achievement records are not sufficient to warrant being recruited away, and their level of drive, ambition, and discipline is sufficiently low so that they are self-described as "content" to stay with the firm.

The selection and effective retention of these "good enough" personnel will lead to the development of a professional force that is largely mediocre in terms of marketing the firm's products and services. It is these marginal personnel that form the largest drag on any organization. If individuals are not carefully selected and finely assessed, then the entire organization can become a mediocre organization. The traditional rule of 20 percent of the work force producing 80 percent of the business is a well-established rubric, but it has its roots in historical records. The corollary of this idea is that 15 percent of some professional work forces do not even pay their own way. The people in this category can take up to 50 percent of the manager's time. So selecting improper personnel is an expensive venture.

A fundamental error frequently made by professional organizations is that they are constantly seeking to select the *already developed* marketing-oriented professional person. This ideal person comes experienced and trained in proven marketing techniques. He or she is disciplined, energetic, socially aggressive, and incentive motivated. He is knowledgeable about the product, educated, or licensed/certified, intelligent and a self-starter. He possesses and readily demonstrates a high degree of self-motivation and drive. The ideal person works well with existing clients and readily markets products/services to new clients. In fact, he or she performs about all the work tasks with equal ease—as proven by a record of success. This person is also ready to work for the organization at any time. In brief, he is almost perfect.

Generally speaking, there are two chances that such a person will walk into the office: slim and none. The reason for this is fairly obvious. Any such person is already profitably employed. He is not looking for a position—especially at his current level within a new firm. He is probably a successful manager of other professionals in a competing firm, or is an independent business owner. This person can be recruited to join your firm—for a price. In fact, the price is generally higher than initially thought, and worst of all, the presumed quality of the person can be lower than was perceived in the recruiting process. Why does this happen? In general, consultants leave their current companies for one of two reasons: 1) The company is no longer providing the type of service/product that the consultant is specialized in providing; or 2) The consultant is dissatisfied with the current firm (generally for reasons that are valid and critical to him), and he feels the need to change. In the first case, the consultant is about to be terminated. Presumably his client list is small and his book of business is at best only marginally profitable. If the consultant controlled a large book of profitable business, the firm would probably not be discontinuing the product/service involved. Second, if the consultant were especially effective, the firm would find some other role for him to fill within the organization.

If a firm is discontinuing a product or service and also the employment of the consultant, then the candidate has little negotiating power with a potential new employer. His lead time is too short. Clients who use the current service will want and need new service fairly quickly. They will be nervous, and despite the consultant's promises to properly service the business, clients will be eager for stable and permanent relationships with a new firm. Moreover, the news that the company is withdrawing from a certain segment of the business is probably being heard "on the street," and personnel from many consulting firms will be actively seeking those clients. The second case, when the professional consultant is dissatisfied with his present firm, is somewhat different. On the surface, the reasons can appear simple. The consultant is interested in leaving his present firm (A) for a new firm (B). Given that he is actively planning the change, he will have sufficient time to plan his strategy and make his move. This move will include transferring some of his clients with him to the new firm. In fact, the ability to bring clients with him to a new firm may be part of the attraction that the new firm has for the consultant. Moreover, bringing in a new set of clients that the consultant can control will probably increase his income, status, and prestige at the new firm.

Many client companies *are* willing to change consulting firms. This is true because many clients are primarily loyal to their professional consultant, and only incidentally to the company he or she represents. Many of these clients assume that as long as they continue to receive quality service from the consultant, then the firm with which the consultant is associated is almost immaterial. The wisdom of the client's decision can be debated, but the fact remains that consultants develop relationships with individuals within client companies and vice versa.

The consultant who is dissatisfied with his present firm A, changes to firm B. Coincidentally, or perhaps as a result of planning, the consultant takes clients with him to the new firm. The actual reasons for the consultant to change firms, and the results that are likely to occur to both the consultant and the firms in question, will be examined.

Consultants will provide many (apparently valid) reasons for being dissatisfied with their present employer. These include the lack of 1) sales/technical/administrative support; 2) respect for the consultant's ideas; and/or 3) monetary rewards/perks for the consultant. Despite the level of emotional intensity, earnest conviction, and detailed explanation with which the consultant describes his situation, the most frequent *real* reason for a consultant changing companies and moving business with him or her is to earn a greater income. Other reasons may also influence the decision to leave a firm, but the person who transfers business in this manner is motivated by increased personal financial reward and is operating in a way that is entirely consistent with his behavior style.

The consultant's former and future employers are aware of his motivations. If a consultant is willing to leave his present employer to join another firm, usually he is willing or required to bring some of his clients with him in order to assure himself of a minimal number of billable hours. In essence, the new firm has "bought" the consultant (and his book of business). Sometimes this change can be completed in a way that is profitable for everyone concerned. However, more often than not such transfers have hidden costs. The repercussions of this type of behavior can be far different from those expected. For example, the consultant may not be able to bring all the accounts that he originally intended to bring. The result of this is that he may be overpaid by the firm for a period of time. This happens when he has a contract that stipulates he is paid X dollars regardless of the clients (billable hours) he brings with him. Another repercussion could be that the consultant is seriously *underpaid* for a period of time. This happens when he is paid X dollars based on the number of clients he brings with him from his former company. If he is not able to transfer as many clients as he anticipated, then his income will suffer. Because he is largely a money-motivated person, he becomes something of a disgruntled employee.

A variation on this theme is when the new consultant comes in at a high income and status level relative to the consultants who have been working for the company for a period of years. In general, the new consultant pays his way because of the business he brought with him. However, because the new firm is different from the old, and because there may be some resentment regarding his high income and high status, he may not adjust to the new surroundings. Therefore, the new consultant is profitable as long as his transferred book of business exists, though he may have difficulty forming relationships with existing consultants and may not contribute significantly beyond his initial business.

Another possible negative impact is more subtle. Even if the new consultant is able to bring all the business he anticipated and earns his income and status, problems can still arise. Problems surface because the other longstanding employees in the firm will perceive that the firm is more interested in "buying" people who control blocks of business than in developing consultants internally. Every time an existing consultant is denied the opportunity to participate in a professional meeting or to attend a training program, he or she will think of the money the firm spent on buying an existing book of business—and hiring a high-level, and presumably high-paid new consultant. As a result, existing consultants become increasingly protective of their clients and will start to plan for the day when they can either demand a significant raise from the firm or "sell" themselves and their client contacts to another firm.

Finally, the possibility also exists that the new consultant who left firm A to join firm B, will just as easily leave firm B to join firm C. When this happens the transfer process continues, and he will take the clients he has historically controlled and brought to firm B, as well as any new clients he has developed at firm B. Thus, his old and newly developed business will end up with firm C. That is, until he senses another opportunity to move the business again.

In the case where the consultant is eager to transfer to a new firm for a variety of reasons, the most frequent reason is personal financial gain with the new firm. The next time he receives an equally attractive offer from another firm, he is likely to transfer again. Such people are money-motivated and eager to reward themselves for their individual efforts. Organizational restrictions can be placed on such movements, but this type of behavior is endemic to the money-motivated individual. Nothing is inherently wrong with the individual, but his behavior pattern is established, and it is unlikely to ever change. The best alternative to such practices is to avoid them altogether. As a general rule, do not hire the individual who is willing, eager, and even anxious to transfer business to your firm—for a price. When a legitimate situation involving a transfer of business arrives, it will be obvious because it is atypical. A partial answer to this problem is to build in structural variables that limit the control a consultant has with a client. In sum, these people present problems that have negative consequences, more costly than the immediate revenue they bring to the firm.

ASSESSMENT

The previous chapter introduced a series of seven behavior traits and behavior styles. These descriptions form a base for understanding people and assessing a candidate's level of interpersonal skill. One of the best ways to use the information presented so far is to focus on those key traits that are critical to the candidate's success with the firm. These traits are primarily manifested in terms of self-discipline as evidenced by the candidate's level of the overachiever trait. They are also demonstrated by an overall drive, as evidenced by high levels of the entrepreneur, active, and aggressive traits. The degree to which a person possesses these traits can be determined in an interview and from reviewing the candidate's personal and work background. Such a review would reveal that certain items in a person's background are indicative of the type of self-discipline, drive, energy, and social aggressiveness he or she possesses. The following highly abbreviated list is designed to assist in understanding and recognizing those traits in candidates.

Item	Indicators
Sports	Determine what he achieved and why it was important to him. Look for a determination to excel; a commitment to excellence; initiative above expectations.
Extra-Curricular Achievement	Boy Scout or Cub Scout leader, team captain; honor society, class officer, student positions, government leader, officer in hobby clubs or civic activities. Distinguish between participation and accomplishment in these areas. In and of themselves, none of the above denote a high level of self-discipline—they are clues so look for a pattern.
Employment	Determine what he has accomplished that is above the expectation for the job or is above and beyond the job description. (This is a good question to use with reference checks.) Look for promotions within and achievement potential of the job itself; sales is more openly competitive than computer programming (usually).
Military	A discharge rank or grade higher than usual considering the length of service could be an indication of discipline.

Academic   Grades in school could be an indication of achieve-
                            ment drive. However, the following should be con-
                            sidered when evaluating grades in school:

                            1. The correlation between Grade Point Average
                            (GPA) and intelligence is not high.

                            2. The correlation between GPA and later success is
                            not high.

                            3. The correlation between GPA and motivation to
                            get good grades is high.

                            4. School is typically a well-structured experience.
                            Some people are motivated to obtain good grades in
                            study, comply, and regurgitate information and there-
                            by do well. Some of these people cannot do nearly as
                            well in a non-academic setting.

                            5. Some do poorly in a very structured environment
                            like school, particularly if at the same time they view
                            the degree requirements as not meaningful or related
                            to their interests.

Aspirations   Highly disciplined, achievement-oriented people
                            generally have a more well-defined set of expecta-
                            tions. There usually exists a more well-defined plan
                            and method to their efforts.

Personal   Energy is constructively directed, more energetic
                            people tend to accomplish more.

Characteristics   Competitiveness. Achievers want to win and be
of Achievers   measured. Look for examples of competitive activities.

                            Independence. Achievers typically learn to rely on
                            themselves earlier. They are self-reliant and take re-
                            sponsibility for their own success or failure.

                            Tenacity. They respond to a challenge rather than
                            make excuses for failure or non-action.

                            Initiative. They tend to make things happen rather
                            than react to what happens.

                            Risk. They are usually more willing to take risks.

                            Desire to influence. There is considerable evidence
                            to indicate that the desire to influence, which de-
                            rives from their power motive, results in a much more

effective management style than does the achievement drive per se. The achiever will accomplish a lot, but the influencer will try to get others to achieve. Look for efforts on the part of the individual to get himself into a position of influence.

The importance of the individual's being in these positions is determined by the reasons he achieved the positions and what he does in those positions, rather than just the fact that he achieved the positions.

Things most proud of in life	The achiever will typically give achievements in responses (won contest; first in class; first in a race; won county tennis tournament) rather than to note areas that might be personally satisfying but less achievement oriented, for example, proud of family; graduated from college; was a Cub Scout; made $25,000 salary.
Nature of Work	Kind of work done or preferred indicates energy, which, as noted above, is a requirement for achievement. Hence, energy is indicated more by outside sales (versus inside sales); truck driving (versus sorting mail); factory work (versus bank work). Remember, these are generalities and are not always true.
What like most about work?	More energy is indicated by action responses like doing, achieving, solving versus opportunity to learn, pleasant surroundings, or friendly associates.

This evaluation process is further enhanced in the interview. A series of interview topics are presented here to better enable the interviewer to understand and assess each candidate in terms of the seven behavior traits. The actual questions related to these topics are listed. This list is followed by a discussion of how each of the seven behavior types typically respond to the questions.

SELF-ESTEEM

In its simplest form, self-esteem is a belief in yourself, your profession, and your ability to perform your work well. No matter what level you start at or achieve in the company, you have to believe in yourself at each level to effectively function at that level. Some questions to help determine a candidate's level of self-esteem are:

1. How would you describe your character?
2. What is the latest challenge you have met?
3. In what ways have you disappointed yourself?

RISK TAKING

Risk taking is the ability to make balanced, rational, and defensible decisions with *incomplete* information. It is an additional measure of a person's self-confidence. Some questions to assist you in determining a candidate's attitude about risk taking are:

1. On a scale of 1 to 10, how much of a risk taker are you? Then no matter what the answer, ask some of the following questions.
2. To be successful as a consultant what percentage of your decisions must be correct?
3. Describe a recent decision having more than the usual element of risk?
4. Tell me about the most risky decision you ever made? What was the situation? How long did it take you to gather the information to make a decision? Was your decision correct?

DRIVE

Drive is a measure of a person's persistence in the face of adversity, his or her determination to accomplish the task at hand regardless of the circumstances. Some sample questions to assist you in determining a candidate's level of drive are:

1. What is success to you?
2. What are your aspirations?
3. What have you done to increase your level of responsibility in your present position?
4. How do you know when you have done a good job?

STRESS TOLERANCE

Stress is an inherent condition of the sales process. The average client-development consultant who denies the existence of stress in the occupation is seldom employed for long in a client-development role. The successful person is one who can and does effectively channel this stress into useful energy. Some questions to help you determine a candidate's level of stress tolerance are:

1. What kinds of problems annoy you the most?
2. Under what conditions do you work best?
3. What, if anything, causes you to lose your temper?

ADAPTABILITY

Adaptability is generally defined as the ability to remain flexible and accept change in the business. This means possessing the maturity to work with other consulting and administrative personnel. This is especially true in the professional services business, where the only thing that is constant is change. Everyone should learn to accept this state of affairs. Some questions to help you measure a person's ability to adapt to change are:

1. How do you handle a difficult client?
2. Give me an example of an instance when you disagreed with your boss. How was it handled?
3. How long does it take you to become comfortable in a new place?

OVERACHIEVER

Self-esteem. The overachiever's level of self-esteem is at the heart of his self-confidence in the selling process. He tends to see himself as a somewhat direct, no-nonsense, purposeful individual. He meets challenges head on and tends to be proud of his conservative bent. At the same time, he may be slightly self-effacing about his accomplishments. He has learned from early in his childhood that bragging is not proper, and the interviewer may have to entice him to talk about some of his larger accomplishments. He sees himself on the verge of completing something important and will tend to indicate that he only really needs a solid opportunity to make his mark. He will generally be accepting of some form of delayed gratification or payment and will eagerly project an image of "Let me show you what I can do for you *before* you invest too much in me." He may then sheepishly add words to the effect, "You may be surprised with what I can do."

Risk Taking. The overachiever may be described as a "cautious" risk taker. He may politely decline to bet on games of pure chance—with the explanation that he cannot influence the outcome. This is the underlying approach that the overachiever has to risk taking. The amount of risk he is willing to accept is in direct proportion to the amount of control he has over the outcome. The more control he *perceives* he has, the more risk he is willing to accept. If he thinks that by virtue of his own dedication, energy, and self-discipline that he can reasonably expect to control the results of a business opportunity—like a position in consulting—then he will eagerly accept the responsibility to deliver. Otherwise, he will refuse.

This suggests that the overachiever *may* need to be sold on the idea that he can directly control his future and his ability to earn money in consulting—especially if he is inexperienced. However, his habits of what he would call "responsible" risk taking should be evident in his interview comments. He wants to win, by playing according to the rules and by allowing his own disciplined work habits to tip the scale in his favor.

Drive. The overachiever is a study in dedication to task accomplishment. However, his emotional intensity is *not always* readily obvious. He is internally driven to achieve and is interested in monitoring his own progress according to norms and indicators that are important to him. He will readily agree to abide by the minimal standards of performance, but he will generally insist (at first to himself and later to his boss) on surpassing them for his own satisfaction. This may seem like a small distinction, but the perception that he is *internally* regulating his behavior is important to him.

Stress Tolerance. The overachiever has a high level of stress tolerance and effectively channels his anxiety into tangible accomplishments. He is capable of working with significant levels of stress. He can deal with the large-scale problematic issues that surface in the consulting process. Conversely, it is a series of "small" mistakes that can cause him to lose his temper. He shows little patience with those people who cannot, will not, or do not prepare for their appointments. His Boy Scout philosophy of "Being Prepared" means that if he anticipates the "little" tasks of the consulting process, the successful accomplishment of the bigger tasks should almost automatically fall into place. He lives by the philosophy that success is a matter of executing the fundamentals of the game.

Adaptability. If the overachiever has a (comparative) weakness, it is probably in the area of adaptability. The internally driven sense of focus, determination, and channeled ambition that make him such a desirable salesperson can also limit his ability to easily change his course of behavior in midstream. His primary rule of thumb is "stay the course," and once a well-prepared plan is implemented, he prefers to see it through to some reasonable conclusion. He tends to see change as weakness, and he may need to be counseled on the need to accept differences in plans once the action begins. He is not so much limited by tunnel vision, as he is concerned about changes that simply make things different.

ENTREPRENEUR

Self-esteem. Almost more than any other behavior type the entrepreneur has an overabundance of self-esteem. All of it may not necessarily be valid, but he certainly possesses it. The more self-disciplined the entrepreneur, the more he deserves credit for his own self-described accomplishments. The entrepreneur is generally not self-effacing in describing his greatest glories. He will do this in a quasi matter-of-fact manner that can hide the pride that generally surrounds most of his stated accomplishments.

He can describe significant challenges where he alone was responsible for turning around difficult situations and reversing a potential loss into a significant profit. However, if prodded, he will generally relate that he did receive some administrative assistance from his co-workers. He may have a difficult time remembering any failure and may say something like, "In all honesty I don't think I have failed at anything yet." The surprising aspect of this statement is how earnestly he can deliver the phrase.

Risk Taking. Risk is almost the entrepreneur's middle name. He is generally ready for a wager on most things. This is part of his get-rich-quick perception of the world. He wants to earn his money before his time is up, and he is eager and sometimes even anxious to partake of the winnings. Unfortunately, he tends to bet more on himself—without proper support—than is warranted by the situation. The result is that although he makes a good impression, he cannot deliver the results on time or within budget. For this reason, he needs to be supervised fairly closely, and under these conditions he can be an effective risk taker. During the interview he will gladly explain, define, and extol the virtues of risk behavior and will freely supply examples of when his "business insights," in terms of accepting risk in a deal, have paid off handsomely.

Drive. The entrepreneur shows a good deal of drive. However, it is generally focused on activities where he can individually and personally harness his energies, skills, and talents for some single victory. He is driven in the competitive sense of the word, but his level of sustained drive can quickly lapse if he is not continuously rewarded for his efforts. He will generally reference some form of competition when discussing the issues of drive, ambition, and task accomplishment. The entrepreneur tends to believe that the best reward for a task well done is money, and he likes to be able to control (in some manner) how he can be rewarded for his unique contribution. Like the professional athlete, who enjoys team victory but insists on keeping a separate set of his individual statistics, the entrepreneur generally is driven in a selfish manner.

Stress Tolerance. The entrepreneur will portray that he deals with stress quite effectively. However, as the temperature rises, his behavior tends to become increasingly self-preservational. He will probably indicate that he works best under conditions where the work requirements are clearly stated and the rewards are simply defined. For him, this means that, "If I do X work then I receive Y reward." This simple system makes great intuitive sense to him, and he can be greatly and honestly surprised that it does not have universal appeal for everyone. He loses his temper primarily when rewards promised to him are not forthcoming, or when the commission structure for his compensation is changed mid-year. The more mature entrepreneur will accept the fact that his compensation plan will often be changed at year end, but he cannot abide mid-stream changes.

Adaptability. The entrepreneur is quite adaptable in appearance and in terms of social decorum. He can readily change his presentation style to fit the needs of the audience. He can also adapt to new business situations and strives to put on the best possible face for situations. He is inherently persuasive, flexible, and adaptable to the changing business environment. He may not like the new deal, but he will generally endorse it—at least until he makes a new arrangement for himself. He is the least likely to openly complain but also the first to jump ship if he perceives that a situation is turning against him.

ACTIVE

Self-esteem. The person typified by the active behavior style generally shows a solid degree of self-esteem. Remember, the active by definition is emotionally charged and likes other people. Almost by definition, he likes himself and feels good about his ability to complete his assignments. However, this self-esteem may not be immediately obvious until the pressure begins to mount to complete a project on time and within budget. The controlled active will say to himself, "It's time to put myself into high gear and get rolling." This will generally translate into behavior that is focused, energized, and directed at accomplishing a series of meaningful goals.

In spite of being asked about "character," the active will respond with a comment that he is a team-oriented, enthusiastic person. He wants to win and complete projects as part of a group effort. He may initially define his character as happy, rather than in moralistic terms. He meets challenges frequently and is generally frustrated when he is not able to complete all his projects, although he will give each of them his best effort. As you might expect, his disappointments come from this occasional failure to complete a task.

Risk Taking. The active person is in favor of risk taking—for the fun of it. He is easily motivated to partake of activity that includes some excitement and frivolity. He is less inclined to see risky ventures as possessing significant amounts of danger or the possibility of loss. He sees these possibilities as part of a great adventure. He is interested in experiencing life to the fullest, and he realizes that he will experience some failures along the way. But he will be quick to add that, "If you don't try to stretch yourself, you will never grow." And for him, a risky situation would be considered an opportunity to grow emotionally. Generally, he will describe situations that involve some form of group activity. He may imply that he was just "swept along" with the crowd and went along for the fun of it. The actual outcome is less important to him than the thrill of the group experience.

Drive. The active does possess a good deal of emotional drive. However, he sometimes needs to be appropriately supervised and channeled to effectively use this trait for his own and his group's benefit. In response to questions about drive during the interview, the active will imply that he wants to do more, but he may only have a vague definition of how to define the word *more*. He is ambitious, and he understands the balance of putting a lot into his work in order to reap the rewards of the sale. He possesses enormous energy potential, but he sometimes needs to be placed in the right environment to convert that potential energy into a kinetic result.

Stress Tolerance. The active person generally shows a strong ability to deal with stress. However, under conditions that create continued pressure, his first negative behavioral reaction will be to increase his activity level—without necessarily increasing his level of work output. He will relate that his most frustrating problems seem to revolve around details, administrative follow-up, and concentrating his energies on *completing* a given task. He has no problem starting assignments, but he sometimes becomes distracted when deadlines approach and he cannot complete his portion of the task on time. For the most part, he will be candid in describing these limitations in his temperament, but he will also indicate that he is terrific at starting and working on projects that have more flexible deadlines. Any candidate that possesses this insight and candor in explaining his own behavior can be effectively supervised for his benefit and the organization's.

Adaptability. Social adaptability and interpersonal flexibility are at the cornerstone of the active's behavior style. Almost anything that happens in a social setting (except hard feelings directed toward a group member) is permissible to him. He is known for his ability "to roll with the punches" and to adapt his schedule to meet the demands of others. However, if others misuse his sense of compromise and abuse his ability to refit his schedule or priorities to accommodate theirs, he can become frustrated and disgruntled. He prides himself on being able to adapt to new social and physical surroundings. He wants to have a reasonable chance to fit in and be appreciated by the members of the group.

PASSIVE

Self-esteem. In general the passive person has a low degree of self-esteem. He is prone to rate his abilities as low, understate his qualifications, and perform in such a way that reinforces the perception that he is "slow" at completing his assignments. Hence, the image reinforces the behavior, and the consequence is that he comes to see himself as a middle-level functionary, but not a leader.

Risk Taking. The passive person prefers to engineer most risk out of situations before embarking on an activity. He is known for making extensive plans, checking lists twice, and re-analyzing his assumptions before starting any action. Moreover, he is most comfortable in making decisions that involve a "group decision." In this way, he can share the potential blame for anything that goes wrong. Since he is not especially interested in claiming the singular credit for successful operations, this is fine with him.

Drive. Since he lacks significant emotional energy, the passive person is generally perceived to possess little drive. He will be productive if adequately controlled by some outside force, but he prefers to combine his efforts with those of others rather than start an action at his own bequest.

Stress Tolerance. The passive person has a low stress tolerance. He dislikes ambiguity and needs and responds best to a set structure, defined rules, and consistency.

Adaptability. Although he feels a great deal of compassion for others who may be experiencing some difficulty with a given situation, he is personally not very adaptable to change himself. He will freeze—mostly out of honest fear of change—rather than readily adapt to a changing situation. He may be shown quite empirically that his current situation is untenable, but he will still have difficulty moving or changing his situation. He is not being consciously stubborn or deliberately resisting the new behavior for some specific reason; he is just afraid of change—no matter what the reason.

SENSITIZED

Self-esteem. The sensitized person possesses a high but generally fragile amount of self-esteem. He prefers to isolate himself from negative input and can filter information he receives about himself to such a degree that primarily positive opinions are perceived. He thinks highly of himself, but he also realizes that he is living a semi-protected existence. He is aware that he can be affected by contrary information, so he may shut himself off from it. He is self-aware and knows that he is socially different (in the sense of being introverted and shy), but he tends to see these characteristics as a strength and mark of uniqueness.

Risk Taking. The sensitized person is not especially risk prone. He may take intellectual risks, and play games in his head, but emotionally, socially, and financially he is generally quite conservative. He sees little value in overtly risky behavior, especially when he can enjoy all the adventure he wants in his own imagination.

Drive. The sensitized person can appear to lack significant drive. However, when focused on an issue or technical problem that interests him, he can be accurately described as a classic workaholic. Once he is intrigued by some esoteric issue of unique importance to him, he will push himself to incredible lengths to finish his task. He tells himself that he is not performing for any tangible or outside reward, but that he is working for the sheer internal pleasure of finding a solution to the given problem. So it is not money, power, or status that drives him, but the desire to accomplish a task for the pleasure of seeing if he can do it.

Stress Tolerance. The sensitized person's reaction to stress can be quite different than expected, and it can vary from one highly sensitized person to another. Frequently, it will take one of two very different forms. Under stress, the person will either wilt and "cave-in" fairly quickly to the pressure of the moment and generally show little ability to deal with the source of stress, or he will act in just the opposite manner and demonstrate an incredible amount of personal and emotional strength. In the latter case, he will accept increasingly heavy loads of pressure and stress, and internalize the feelings of discomfort he is experiencing.

Adaptability. The sensitized person can have difficulty adapting to rapid change, but his behavior can be quite different during a change process. In such circumstances, he may become unattached to anything and adapt as if nothing mattered to him. He will be apparently happy to live with whatever change is mandated for him. In this case, he will blithely say, "My input is immaterial and whatever will happen will happen, so I might as well go along with it." Or, he can adopt an opposite approach and attempt to stonewall any efforts to include him in the change process. If this happens, he may deliberately but quite secretly sabotage the effort to accomplish a successful change.

AGGRESSIVE

Self-esteem. The aggressive person believes in himself, his purpose, and his ambitions. He tends to be a very focused and goal-driven person. He will openly describe his character as strong-willed and can generally recite an instance where he had to persevere to overcome objections and obstacles to gain a specific end. He is proud of the fact that he has overcome setbacks and sees each victory as a stepping stone to further challenge. His ego is firmly intact, and he believes in his ways and suggests that his record of accomplishment should speak for his self-esteem.

Risk Taking. In general the primarily aggressive person prefers to avoid random risk. He sees little value in betting on gambling events like horse racing, sports events, and the like. This is in contrast to the entrepreneur-aggressive person who willingly bets on such events. The aggressive will wager money on events where he is personally involved and where he feels his personal input can make a significant difference. He strives to engineer the risk portion of any event to a minimum by extensive preparation and contingency planning. In this way, he feels prepared to face most alternative decision points along the way. After all, he is suspicious of people and events, and the best way to allay those feelings is with thorough planning and anticipation.

Drive. By almost anybody's definition, the aggressive person is highly driven. He is frequently cited as the individual who made the critical difference in the success of a given operation. The aggressive's focused determination, perseverance, and channeled energy are generally obvious to others. He is not so much a workaholic, as he is a methodically forward-moving machine that seldom stops for obvious nurturance or rest. He can be called overly ambitious, but also driven.

Stress Tolerance. The aggressive person has difficulty understanding disagreements with his plan, purpose, and results. He is generally convinced of the "rightness" of his approach, and although he will listen to the opinions of others, he frequently charges ahead, relying primarily on his own perceptions of an issue. When frustrated at the lack of progress on a project, which can happen often, he will become visibly upset. At such times he is verbally upset and increasingly demanding of his subordinates. He sees himself as living with deadlines, and he expects others to do the same.

Adaptability. The aggressive can adapt to changing situations—if he has to—but he prefers that others accommodate him. In his own office and immediate environment, he can become fixated on establishing set routines to follow, and he may insist on rules of order that seem cumbersome and outdated. Because he is the boss, he will demand compliance with his wishes. However, when dealing with others who are not under his control, but to whom he is eager to sell something, he can be quite charming and persuasive. This behavior will generally last as long as required by the situation, but ultimately he will return to his more control-oriented self. His answers to questions about adaptability will truthfully vary. He can be very flexible in some situations, but in others he will stubbornly insist on having his way.

COMPULSIVE

Self-esteem. The compulsive person holds a high, but not especially public, opinion of himself. He is less concerned with supervisory ratings, peer review, or objective measures of his performance. He is focused on task accomplishment. Given that he generally completes whatever he begins in the time frame that he established for himself, he generally has a positive but not showy opinion of himself.

Risk Taking. The compulsive person will eagerly compute the odds of a given event occurring, but he is less interested in actually placing a wager on the outcome. High risk taking in the form of gambling is not his activity of choice. If he sees where he has a clear edge, he may risk something, but primarily to prove the fact that he could control the risk. For example, the compulsive person is more likely to create a ranking system for professional sports teams that would give the "betting odds" for picking one team over another. He *may* be inclined to bet on the teams his system favors to validate his choice in hard currency. However, his primary pleasure would be in creating the system and observing its accuracy in predicting success or failure.

Drive. The compulsive person is sometimes compared to a train that moves at a constant 40 miles per hour. This may be considered an indication of a low level of drive. However, the compulsive person (train) runs at this speed in all conditions, at all times. He never slows down in spite of the obstacles he is facing, and he always produces at a constant rate. He is driven to accomplish solid goals, especially over time.

Stress Tolerance. In some ways the compulsive person's apparently low emotionality enables him to work with a constant sense of determination under even significant levels of stress. If asked how he does it (works under highly stressful conditions of time, complicated problems, etc.), he would probably respond, "Being emotional under such conditions is simply a waste of energy."

Adaptability. The compulsive person can be accused of not being readily adaptable to changing work conditions. He prefers to work on projects sequentially, one at a time. He can change his focus from one task to another, but it is not his preferred approach. To ask him to operate in a multi-task environment can limit his task effectiveness and increase his sense of frustration.

CONCLUSION

Understanding the traits, like any new skill, will increase with practice. Try thinking of people you know in terms of these traits and define their overall behavior patterns using the seven traits. More importantly, define potential professional marketing personnel in terms of the traits, and record specific incidents from their background or interview comments that indicate a score of high, medium, or low on a given trait. This process will require time, but it will be immensely useful. Describing a person's trait patterns will enable you to better understand and manage him or her, more accurately describe him or her to another person, and to make more effective hiring decisions.

Understanding the relationships between and among the traits begins with recognizing the *primary* importance of the overachiever trait. The overachiever is the most critical of all the traits. It operates as a separate and independent function in determining a person's behavior style. It also influences the other traits in the total pattern. In general, if the overachiever is low, then the person may be described as lacking self-discipline and emotional control. He may act on his impulses more readily and attempt to satisfy his more immediate needs without significant consideration of others' needs.

In essence, the overachiever trait acts as a control switch for the other six traits. In general, the higher the overachiever score, the more reliable the person and the better controlled the entire behavior style. For these reasons, it is important to be able to perceive, read, and evaluate candidates in terms of the amount of this trait that they possess. The amount of the overachiever trait present in the behavior style will ultimately determine whether the person has the discipline, integrity, and perseverance needed to be successful with the company.

The traits do not combine additively to form a unique behavior style. Typically, a person can be characterized by focusing on two to three traits. First, identify the amount of overachiever in his behavior, and then identify the one or two additional traits that highlight his behavior. Some examples of these combinations follow:

Active-Passive. The active and passive behavior types are frequently combined in an individual in a variety of degrees and will be discussed jointly here. Although they are frequently found together, it is not uncommon to find an active without much of the passive trait; or a strict passive without significant amounts of the active. The active behavior type is readily recognized due to the person's overall cheerfulness, enthusiasm for whatever activity he is engaged in, and genuine warmth for the people he is dealing with. The active-passive may show periods of reduced activity from time to time, but generally will marshall whatever energy is necessary in order to accomplish whatever task has been assigned.

When the active individual lacks self-control, his enthusiasm is likely to become irksome to the more serious members of the organization, and his untiring desire for fun and frivolity will discourage the most loyal friends. As the control diminishes, he will begin to show periods of moodiness and downheartedness. His overall performance will be impaired by periods of both elation and depression. His mood will become apparently unpredictable and increasingly irksome to his fellow employees.

When the two traits (active and passive) are present in a person's makeup to an equal degree, it results in an individual who is at times positive, optimistic, cheerful, and industrious, and at other times downhearted, moody, grouchy, and sullen. The actual amount of time spent in the two moods varies from one individual to the next, so that all manner of combinations are possible. An apparently happy, outgoing person's mood may quickly change to conservatism and nit-picking without apparent reason or cause.

Frequently, the active-passive behavior type will start his day feeling tired and barely able to meet the minimal requirements of the day, but after a cup of coffee and some self-prodding, he becomes an unstoppable bundle of energy, taking responsibility and looking into projects. The active-passive is really a cyclic behavior pattern, with frequent changes in the aspect that is showing itself at any given time.

Figure 4.1
Self-Rated Description of Your Behavior Style

SEVEN TRAITS	CATEGORY								
	LOW			MEDIUM			HIGH		
	1	2	3	4	5	6	7	8	9
Overachiever									
Entrepreneur									
Active									
Passive									
Sensitized									
Aggressive									
Compulsive									

Explanation/Definition of Rating:

Self-Esteem: _____

_____

Risk-Taking: _____

_____

Drive: _____

_____

Stress Tolerance: _____

_____

Adaptability: _____

_____

Active-Aggressive. The person who demonstrates an active-aggressive behavior style encourages team attitudes. He helps his group surpass its competition. He reduces money motives in the interest of team recognition. His suggestions about advertising and marketing are innovative. He offers superiors ideas. He is helpful to fellow consultants. He subordinates personal gain for the benefit of the group. He has the courage and strength to implement and support corporate change. He meets customer complaints and impatience in positive ways. He does not rationalize a customer's brush off and looks for a new approach. In fact, he hardly ever takes the first "no" as being final.

He displays the judgment, flexibility, and openness that allow him to admit errors and the ego to claim a significant share of the credit for group accomplishment. The active-aggressive consultant not only accepts change but invites and initiates it. He does not leave when a situation is difficult since he is skilled in turning adversity into success and stagnation into action.

Overachiever-Entrepreneur. The overachiever-entrepreneur is disciplined, controlled, and driving in his need to competitively "win" at most endeavors. He sees himself as either winning or losing on a daily basis.

Entrepreneur-Aggressive. The entrepreneur-aggressive seeks to attain a position of power and influence in the organization. Money is his yardstick of success. He is competitive, hard working, and goal oriented.

Overachiever-Active-Passive. The overachiever-active-passive is genuinely team oriented, cheerful, outgoing, and well meaning, but he is also controlled and deliberate in his use of energy and emotions. He prefers to work in an emotionally positive environment, but he will be productive anywhere.

Test your understanding of the traits and yourself using Figure 4.1. Graph yourself on the chart and explain your reasoning, in terms of the traits covered in the chapter (self-esteem, risk taking, drive, stress tolerance, and adaptability). Show your chart and explanation to other people who have read this text and see if they agree with you. Follow the same procedure for them. Ask them to chart themselves and describe themselves in writing in terms of the traits and then review their analysis and compare it with your own viewpoint. Using this chart will enable you to better understand the traits in order to identify candidates who are more likely to succeed in the firm. Three key ideas will enable you to effectively use the information: 1) Understand the traits themselves; 2) recognize the relationships between and among the traits; and 3) devise some shorthand mechanisms for identifying the candidate's behavior style.

Chapter Five

ENLISTMENT

Enlistment is the last step in the recruitment process. Due to its importance, it occupies an entire chapter in this book. This phase should be thought of as the final act of wooing the potential candidate into the firm. Just as more experienced and higher-level professional service personnel market themselves (and the firm) to new clients, they should market themselves and the firm to new candidates. It is not sufficient to merely select and finely assess good people to join the firm. These individuals must be sold on the idea of joining the firm. After all, if the firm finds a given candidate attractive for a position, other organizations will probably come to a similar conclusion.

If the preceding selection and assessment steps have been carefully handled, then the enlistment step should be the easiest part in the entire program. Under ideal conditions, the candidate demonstrates the intelligence, technical knowledge, and interpersonal skills necessary to perform the job functions. Consequently, he is made an offer and accepts. Frequently, however, the conditions are not perfect. Occasionally, some of the best candidates are "lost" at this step in the process. This is unfortunate for a number of reasons, principally because the longer the company interviews a candidate the more expensive the process becomes. For example, travel, hotel accommodations, meals, advertising expenses, and, perhaps most importantly, the valued time of firm members, all contribute to this expense. The candidate also will have a fair amount of emotional energy invested in the process. If the candidate is told at the apparent "last moment" that the firm is not interested in him, this can be a disheartening experience. If the recruitment process is not successful at this stage, for whatever reason, then time, money, and emotional energy have each been misspent.

If the candidate reveals some unforeseen problematic issue about himself at the last moment, then clearly the firm is better off not making him an offer. Conversely, if the candidate himself discovers some inherent condition in the firm that will lead to a poor match, then he, too, is wise to stop the process. If either of these conditons could have been detected earlier, then some amount of expense and time could have been saved, and this is better for both the candidate and the firm.

Whatever the reason(s) for an unsuccessful match, it is generally wise to maintain a professional and respectful relationship with the candidate. He or she may know of other individuals who would be better suited to the firm—and be happy to refer them based on the treatment he received. Or the firm may wish to reconsider the person's candidacy at some later time. It is an old, but frequently seen, axiom that bad news seems to travel faster than good news. So if a candidate is treated (in his eyes) poorly, he is more likely to spread the word among his peers and associates. The obvious lesson is to handle everyone's candidacy with the level of professionalism and polite discretion that you would expect and appreciate.

The enlistment process begins at the start of the selection process. How well the enlistment process was conducted cannot be determined until the end of the process with each candidate—when he or she will either accept or reject the offer. However, it is important to recognize that the enlistment process begins and takes place *throughout* the entire candidate review process. Each part of the process influences the final outcome. Most candidates do not "finally" decide that they will or will not join the firm. They make a series of intermediate judgments at each step in the process. The members of the firm may rightfully feel that they are interviewing the candidate, but better candidates will also candidly or subtly interview the firm! It is a two-way process.

The better prepared the firm is to read and interpret the stated and implied interests of each candidate, the more likely the firm is to hire the better candidates. Just as in selling the firm's products and services to existing and new clients, the better prepared firm frequently makes the sale. It should be clearly understood that hiring better people is, in part, a sales process.

The key to the successful enlistment of a candidate is to understand, analyze, and even sell to the individual behavior style of the candidate. Most candidates will want to feel a sense of "fit" between their level of knowledge, skill, and ability and the needs of the firm. However, each candidate, defined as a different behavior style, will emphasize some unique aspect of the firm that is especially important to him or her. The firm must be aware of these subtle messages and respond accordingly to meet the perceived needs of the candidate. For example, some candidates are motivated by the opportunity for factors as diverse as increased self-development, more money, or enlarged social power. Others will be induced to join the firm for other reasons.

Obviously, the firm cannot change its recruiting posture or modify its overall culture in a half-hearted attempt to win over some particular candidate. This would be shortsighted and foolish. If a basic fit between the candidate and the firm does not exist, then any possible masquerade will probably result in a short period of employment. Such behavior is clearly a recipe for disaster. However, to the extent possible, the members of the firm can stress the characteristics of the firm that are important to the candidate. This is a simple matter of emphasis, not distortion. Discussing subjects and concerns that are important to the candidate and are also important to the firm is part of the selling process.

Alternatively, the candidate can be told that the firm is in a period of transition, and that currently the firm and he may not have an ideal fit, *but* that people like him are needed in the firm to assist in this changeover. The candidate would then be facing a "ground-floor" opportunity to rebuild the firm in a new direction. For example, senior members of the firm can openly tell a candidate that his behavior style is different from the typical member in the firm and that this is quite positive. The senior firm members can then communicate that they believe the candidate's behavior style is exactly what is needed to change the firm and that although the person may initially be perceived as somewhat different from the other members of the firm, senior management is committed to hiring more people just like him or her. In other words, the firm can legitimately sell the candidate on the firm during the entire recruiting process.

The candidate will increasingly reveal himself and his behavior style during the interview process. The reason that the interview process is a good place to evaluate the candidate's behavior style is because it is an inherently nerve-racking process. Whatever the candidate's level of sophistication or possible entrance level into the firm, the interview process will cause some anxiety. Even the most experienced marketing professionals will show some signs of strain or uneasiness. The more experienced candidates should be the most capable of effectively carrying out this type of presentation with social grace and comparative ease. However, in this situation these senior-level people are "candidates," and they are also being interviewed by senior level personnel at the firm. Presumably they are facing people as equally skilled as they are in terms of interpersonal abilities.

Most candidates will be interviewed more than once and by more than one interviewer. Generally, the more a candidate is interviewed, the more he will reveal himself. Of course, the interviewer(s) must also be observant about the candidate and willing to use their assessments in terms of politely "selling" to the candidate. However, the primary input from the team of interviewers should be to assess and understand the candidate's level of intelligence, technical competence, and interpersonal skills. They should then record and report their impressions of these three areas to the person who is primarily responsible for recruiting the candidate. This is best completed by having each interviewer complete the Candidate Profile Evaluation Rating Form, as shown in Figure 5.1. The "primary recruiter" can then use the information listed on the form, combine it with his own impressions of the candidate, and decide upon the best approach to enlist the candidate. If the collective impressions of the members of the interviewing team are positive, and the firm has decided to definitely enlist the candidate, the real "enlistment process" begins.

The primary recruiter should prepare a plan to meet the candidate's needs, expectations, and aspirations. He or she should then attempt to sell the firm to the candidate. Up to this point, the candidate has been trying to sell himself on the firm. Now the roles should be openly reversed. This process is too important to be merely delegated to a randomly selected person. Neither should it be left entirely to the professional (outside) recruiter. It should be completed by an in-house person. This selling process should not be a "new" skill for most marketing-oriented professionals. Just as experienced professional service personnel learn to market their services and gain an intuitive feeling for a client over time, they can learn to market to and understand a candidate. This is best done by learning to appreciate the candidate's behavior style.

This sales process should be carefully and systematically performed by the primary recruiter who is responsible for bringing the candidate into the firm to be interviewed. This (internal) recruiter is perceived by the candidate as his "internal champion." That champion should purposefully, directly, and with great thoroughness sell the candidate on the idea of joining the firm. This process can last from 1 to 4 hours. It should be carefully structured and follow a detailed plan. This process should include a discussion of the following points:

1. *Definition.* The candidate should have an apppreciation of the history of the firm. This includes founding, growth pattern, and the reason the position is open (new position, termination, transfer, etc.). He should have an understanding and acceptance of his

Figure 5.1
Candidate Profile Evaluation Rating Form

| PROFILE for: _____ |
| Candidate for position level (circle one)   1   2   3   4   5   6 |

| | RATING | | | | | | | | |
| | LOW | | | MEDIUM | | | HIGH | | |
FACTOR	1	2	3	4	5	6	7	8	9
Tech Comp A									
Tech Comp B									
Tech Comp C									
Verbal R									
Numerical R									
Conceptual R									
Overachiever									
Entrepreneur									
Active									
Passive									
Sensitized									
Aggressive									
Compulsive									

job duties and responsibilities. He should also have an appreciation for the people reporting to him (if any) and the people to whom he reports.

2. *People.* The candidate should be made aware of how the firm sees his behavior style and, more importantly, how his style can fit into, contribute to, and be rewarded by the firm.

3. *Processes.* The candidate should be made aware of the firm's manner of conducting internal affairs, including the type of performance appraisal used, the criteria for advancement, the overall management style, and the general form of compensation and benefits.

4. *Structure.* The candidate should learn the corporate design, reporting structure, and the implied culture of the firm. He should have an understanding of the hierarchy of the firm and where he fits in.

Although the enlistment plan will be well scripted and prepared, it should be delivered in a manner that is best suited to each candidate. The exact content should be semi-tailored to the candidate. The result of the process should be that the candidate is eager to join the firm.

The process of understanding and relating to the candidates as individuals while delivering the four-point message outlined above is not easy. It is best performed by taking into consideration that each person is an individual with unique needs and aspirations, and by understanding the candidate's overall behavior style. In this way the candidates will perceive that the firm is providing information for their general and specific needs. By focusing on the candidate's behavior style, and satisfying the candidate's associated needs, the firm will increase the likelihood that the candidate will join the firm.

OVERACHIEVER

The candidate who is the overachiever will be readily apparent. He will demonstrate all the traits and characteristics associated with his well-defined history of disciplined accomplishment. Generally, he will act in a simple, unaffected, and cordial manner. But under the "pressure" of an interview, he may demonstrate more of his characteristic cool and serious demeanor.

A careful definition of the firm (and his place in it) is important to the overachiever. He prides himself on being a rational and logical person. He will want to hear some history of the organization. He is not so much enamored with history per se, nor is he especially impressed with a firm that was founded 100 years ago. He will be impressed with a firm that has a sense of its origins and an established company philosophy on critical issues. He wants to feel that he is joining an "upstanding" (even if young in years) organization.

He is especially interested in learning how the firm responds to pressure. The pressure can come from a variety of sources, but he will want to believe that he is joining a disciplined, conservative, basically solid organization. Historical evidence of how the firm responded to such hard times as economic recessions, lawsuits, loss of major client(s), and the like, can be strangely reassuring to him, that is, if the firm acted in what he considers a responsible and forthright manner.

Defining the overachiever's behavior style shows the candidate that the firm took the time to understand and define him in terms that he sees as important. He will assume that if the firm perceives his set of standards as valuable, then the firm values the same principles in others. In general, he will feel either that he is joining a group of like-minded individuals who share his sense of discipline, or that some of the people with whom he interviewed in the firm are not as disciplined as he is, but that the firm is selecting more disciplined individuals and that he is that new "type" of person. Recognizing the overachiever will vindicate his desire to see the firm as a place that endorses his sense of stability and discipline focused on overcoming any and all obstacles.

The exact internal administrative processes that the firm uses to accomplish its goals will be of some interest to the overachiever. However, it is much more important to him that such processes are in place. He instinctively dislikes the "seat of the pants" approach and feels much more comfortable with some form of standard measurement. He wants to know that reasonably objective, fact-based, and commonly accepted rules and bylaws are in place. He is less concerned with the exact format of the performance appraisal system than he is in hearing that one exists and has been in place for some time. He is not concerned that the form is one or five pages long, and he feels little concern about whether it is a check-the-box stationery store standard or a custom-designed computer diskette. He is interested in the fact that whatever system is used is reliable and valid.

He will be pleased to hear that at least semi-objective criteria exist for advancement. If he is told (and acknowledges) that he must market himself at X dollars per hour for 1,000 hours over the course of the year, that is a requirement that he can accept. However, if he is told that he should "invoice his time as much as possible," he may become somewhat cautious and unsure about the firm's commitment to excellence. He wants to be measured and is willing to compare his accomplishments against anyone's—as long as they are measured objectively. The overachiever recognizes that the measurement process does not have to be set in stone and should be *less* mechanical at the higher levels of the organization. However, he will respond to some form of objectively measured contribution to the firm. He knows that he can operate somewhat mechanically in social situations, and he wants to ensure that his advancement is primarily predicated upon real accomplishment, not less tangible factors like his perceived social style.

The exact structure of the firm is moderately important to him. He assumes that the organization's design is reasonably effective and that he need not bother with it. His philosophy is that the best rise to the top by virtue of hard work and solid accomplishment. So whatever the paper configuration of the reporting relationships, he assumes that his superior record of disciplined accomplishment will be recognized.

He is less concerned with changing the structure, than he is with simply obeying it. Like most incoming people, he will want to know "who's on first," but this interest is to pay reasonable homage to his superiors. He would prefer that the company endorse his sense of discipline and control, and if the company operates in a way that is radically different from his perception of right and wrong (that is, too aggressive or entrepreneurial), he may not be a good fit with the firm. In the case where the firm readily displays an entrepreneurial orientation, the more he can isolate his function from the mainstream of the firm's philosophy, the more likely he will be to join—and make a solid contribution.

ENTREPRENEUR

This person is competitive, driven, achievement-motivated, and ambitious to earn his way to the top in the shortest period of time. He is prone to Machiavellian intrigue and, although generally open about his competitive drive, he can be clever and political in some situations.

The candidate who demonstrates the entrepreneur behavior style may already know some history of the firm. He is not so much interested in history as he is in the financial aspects of the firm. He is the most likely candidate to have checked the firm's reputation on the street, but probably not the library. He will have made a determination about the financial stability of the organization, and he will be interested in hearing the reason for the current opening. He will be the most interested in hearing the reasons why the incumbent "failed" to perform his duties—if he is replacing someone. Whatever the reasons given for his predecessor's failure, he will assume that he can do the job. However, he may use his predecessor's failure as a reason to request additional support services or increased compensation for himself.

His prime interest in his subordinates will be to determine who can work with independence and little emotional support from him. What time he does have available for employee development will be spent with the people who are like him. The others will typically have to fend for themselves. He believes in competition and is quick to advertise this position. He will be especially interested in the individuals who hold positions of power immediately above his position. He will see these people as critical to his success, and he will be eager for information about them.

He will find his behavior profile flattering—especially if it is presented in a positive light. Phrases like, "Yeah, that's me," and, "I'm damn proud of it," will frequently follow these behavioral feedback sessions. At this stage, the behavioral style review should include two fairly distinct areas. The first should emphasize that his particular traits are needed in the firm. The fact that he can make a significant contribution and be financially rewarded for it should be explained. It can be openly admitted that the firm expects him to readily show his promise. The second point also needs to be highlighted: everyone, and especially the senior level firm members who meet him, recognizes his competitive zeal and believes it is important. They see his positive sense of social style and the effect it can have on clients. They also see that his natural sales ability is a quite positive factor in his candidacy.

The candidate should also be told that the firm is a reasonably team-oriented organization (whatever the level of team play that exists in the firm, this statement should be made) and that the firm operates on the highest level of professional ethics and standards as most professional firms do, and although billable hours are one important measure of success in the firm, they are only one indication of contribution. The candidate needs to be told that he may need to rein in his entrepreneurial spirit somewhat in order to effectively work in the firm. As a rule, the entrepreneur will politely listen to this presentation, but it will have negligible effect on his initial behavior once in the firm. He will still operate in a competitive, persuasive, and essentially "selfish" manner.

The entrepreneur will show some interest in the performance appraisal package, primarily in how raises, bonuses, perks, and promotions are calculated. He may be told that part of the evaluation depends on cooperative selling and part depends on individual selling. He will hear the entire presentation but will especially listen to the portion about individual selling. Selling, whether in a team atmosphere or in an individual mode, is his specialty, but he expects to be rewarded for his separate contribution. In all fairness to the entrepreneur, he is less interested in being rewarded for *efforts*, but will demand what he considers to be fair compensation for his *results*. If the firm has a company policy and defined standards for "splitting" sales credit on new business, this policy should be explained to him in *great* detail. The purpose of this is twofold. First, almost any discussion of compensation is of immense interest to the entrepreneur. Second, the firm is saying that it recognizes this trait in his behavior style (money motivation) and that it wants to ensure that he understands the rules about allocation of credit for sales results. Then there will be little or no confusion later about who deserves credit for a given sale. Nonetheless, disputes, minor arguments, and potentially heated discussions are almost certain to follow when settling credit for sales where the entrepreneur is concerned. This is one of the trade-offs when deciding to hire the entrepreneur. It is also part of management's responsibility. The earlier the policies, procedures, and rules are explained to the entrepreneur, the better off everyone will be when this almost inevitable discussion starts.

The corporate structure and hierarchy of the organization are important to the entrepreneur. He is competitive and perceives himself to be on the fast track to stardom. Hence, he is interested in discovering the individuals who hold positions of power. He is eager to ingratiate himself with these people. He will also want to hear about the culture of the firm, and he will hope that it is entrepreneurial, that is, largely sales oriented, bonus driven, and generally rewarding of independent behavior. If the firm demonstrates a "mixed" culture, in that both team- and individual-oriented personnel are rewarded, then he will readily gravitate toward his fellow entrepreneurs. His inclination will be to express camaraderie with his fellow entrepreneurs and to demonstrate some mild, although generally politely masked, disdain for the more team-oriented professionals in the firm.

For this reason, it is especially important that structural variables be fixed. Variables like policies and rules on sharing sales credit, bonus awards, and recognition for new business development should be firmly established and consistently enforced. The entrepreneur is not so much looking for loopholes in the system to improve his lot, as he is merely prone to finding them when they do exist. Given his perception of the world, he is likely to test the strength of any loosely defined policy. Once he understands the inflexible nature of the rules, he will readily abide by them and be a productive professional contributor.

ACTIVE

The active person is the embodiment of team spirit and group effort. If properly directed, he can become the personification of team achievement, as well. He is sociable, outgoing, positive, and readily shows a contagious sense of energy and well-intentioned feeling that can infect the other members of the firm.

The active person can profit from some historical grounding in the traditions of the firm. He is interested in change. Understanding and accepting that the firm has established a certain style and substance will limit his tendency to want to change things. He will be interested in the reasons for the existence of the opening. He will feel some compassion for the person who failed to be successful in the post. He will be most responsive to the idea that the firm is expanding at a rapid rate and created the position to satisfy a newly discovered market niche. Finally, he wants to feel that the firm believes that he is the person to fill the need.

He wants to hear that the purpose of the job is to satisfy client needs and to earn a respectable return on investment. His perception is that the client comes first. He understands that he and the firm need to earn a living by providing a professional service. He will be interested in meeting his peers, superiors, and subordinates. However, he is likely to treat all like peers. His sense of enthusiasm generally allows him to treat everyone as an equal, and he feels that everyone can achieve something together.

The active person will be especially delighted to hear himself described as a positive person. He wants to believe that his own special brand of sharing will be appreciated. He also prefers to think that he can contribute in a significant way to the overall effort. If the firm is entrepreneurial *and* team-oriented (and many firms are both), the active individual will need to understand that not everyone views the firm as a place for egalitarian sharing, although many people do, and he will certainly be treated fairly and with due consideration for his ideas.

The active candidate will politely listen to a description of the internal processes of the firm, but his comments will typically be something like, "So it's pretty much the standard, right?" As this statement implies, he is more interested in meeting the people than he is in working with the structure. He will happily abide by the rules and understands the need for consistency, regulations, and reliable performance. His interest in the rules stems from his desire to know the boundaries so that he will not offend anyone.

The active person is not interested in breaking or even bending any policies to fit his own needs, but he wants to know how far he can go in any given direction before he has to turn in a new direction. He is more than willing to share and achieve in harmony with others, but he will resent being taken advantage of by others. He is the ultimate team player. The active person respects the rights and territories of others, but he expects reasonable due for his contribution to the effort.

The active needs to be made aware of the structure of the firm. He is inclined to talk *with and to* anyone. He does not deliberately ignore the chain of command as much as he innocently bypasses it. He is not being clever or surreptitious in this behavior but is acting in a friendly manner. This kind of behavior can breed resentment among his peers, and he needs to be aware of the political boundaries that he should and should not cross. He assumes that the culture is team oriented and when he learns the nuances of the corporate culture, he will be somewhat disappointed to learn that it is not 100 percent team oriented.

The active needs to understand that he is presently at level x in the marketing-oriented firm and that in order to ascend to the next higher level(s) he needs to succeed at specific types of sales activities. He will readily accept the responsibility for increased sales and will generally fulfill them in a professional manner. However, he does need to be told the structure and rules for increasing sales and prescribed methods for recording his contribution to the sales accomplishments. He is initially inclined to think that this type of administrative record keeping will be performed automatically, and he will be disappointed to learn that he did not receive his reasonable share of credit for a project because he failed to complete some administrative form.

PASSIVE

The person whose behavior style is primarily passive seldom makes a successful marketing-oriented professional service person. He is too cautious, tentative, negative, and even gloomy. The saving grace for the passive trait is that it frequently mixes with the active trait to form the active-passive behavior style. This person's behavior is a combination of the two traits. He is at once funny and sad, outgoing and sociable, but also tentative. He is optimistic but also occasionally moody and even sharp tongued.

This narrowly defined behavior profile may not seem especially compatible with a successful career in a marketing-oriented professional service firm, and when considering only these characteristics, the person may not be especially successful. However, when this behavior style is combined with a high degree of intelligence, sophisticated training, and specialized education, it can make for a formidable package of *overall* behavior. The person can show a rapier-like wit, a sharp mind that quickly focuses on the heart of any matter, and an incredibly humorous and entertaining social presence, all of which can lead to success in marketing professional services. Candidates with this overall profile of behavior traits, plus intelligence and education, are worth studying and considering for enlistment into the firm.

The person whose temperament includes a significant portion of the passive trait will especially appreciate a detailed history of the firm. He is concerned with security, consistency, and reliability. He wants to feel that he is associating with an organization that is stable and dependable, and which will be in existence for some period of time. He may not explicitly express his interest in a historical perspective, but he will be impressed with the fact that one is included in the presentation. Consistent with his cautious approach to change, he will be concerned about the position if the previous incumbent was fired for non-performance. This information will threaten him and cause him to wonder if the organization acted too hastily in firing the predecessor.

If the position is totally new, he may also find a cause for concern because he will assume that exact guidelines will probably not exist for what is expected of him. He has to be gently introduced to and coached through this portion of the enlistment. He will want to know about his position in the hierarchy because he is concerned with order and predictability. Knowing who his superior is and where he stands in the line of authority will be important to him because passive individuals frequently seek the reassurance of their boss in making even simple decisions.

The passive person will enjoy being told that he is partially passive. This will reassure him that the firm is aware of his behavior style and still wants him to join. He will feel comfortable that he is welcome and has been endorsed—even with his occasionally cautious approach to problem solving. He may need to be told to curb his occasional desire to be sarcastic and biting. It should also be mentioned that he needs to discipline himself to ensure that he accomplishes his goals and is not satisfied with merely trying to finish on time. He must, in fact, finish his projects by the deadlines assigned.

The internal processes of the organization are also of interest to him. First and foremost, he wants to know that they are in place, are working, and generally provide consistent results. Such seemingly small items can be a source of comfort to the passive candidate. A strongly entrepreneurial or aggressive management style will simply scare him. He wants to hear of committee meetings, group decisions, and reasonable deliberation before any significant investments are made. These kind of processes should be advertised to him to the extent they exist. This style will provide him with emotional reassurance. For many of the same reasons, he needs to know the organizational structure. He wants to feel comfortable with his place in the organization and know that he will have a reasonably secure niche in the firm. He wants some knowledge of the firm in order to better understand what his position is in relation to others.

SENSITIZED

At first glance the sensitized person seems about as likely to be successful in a marketing-oriented professional services firm as the passive person. Here again, however, looks can be deceiving. The sensitized person is typically quite creative. If this creativity is combined with superior intelligence and educational/work training, then he can be highly effective with clients in some marketing situations. This is especially true when an initial sales contact has been established, and the sensitized person is brought in and casually introduced as the "technical wizard" on a given project. Clients will readily understand and appreciate his unique contribution to a given project and can insist that he be part of any team that works on future projects. They readily accept that he may not be the most socially polished person. Clients will also accept that he is not especially convincing during the primary selling stages of a project. However, they can, and frequently do, come to see the sensitized person as the "creative brains" behind the final products they receive.

Many people who are high on the sensitized trait, combine that score with a high degree of the overachiever. This combination describes a person who is inclined to be shy but who is also incredibly disciplined and who literally forces himself to the forefront of social situations. Under these conditions, although initially somewhat reticent and formal, he is also highly focused, effective, and insightful in solving client problems. Hence, he is very respected, and his involvement is eagerly awaited by clients.

As an alternative, the highly sensitized person also frequently scores high on the active and passive traits. This results in a person whose behavior style is best described as active-passive-sensitized. This means that he is warm, personable, and sociable (active), but also compassionate, well meaning, and sympathetic (passive), and insightful, perceptive, and highly creative (sensitized). When these behavior traits are combined with a high degree of intelligence, education, and training, the *overall* behavior pattern is quite effective. The combination of these traits makes the person a very likeable, but not necessarily socially aggressive person, whose advice is frequently sought by clients and firm associates alike.

The sensitized person may have an academic interest in the firm's history. He may find it interesting but not especially important to him. He will be curious about the reasons for his predecessor's leaving but will not be unduly affected by the stated reasons. He will determine that he can or cannot do the job according to his own level of ability. He seldom compares himself to others, and although socially quiet, he is fiercely independent in his thinking and actions. He will feel compassion for the person who lost his job, but the fact that someone could not do the work has no relevance to his self-perceived ability to complete the assignment.

Relaying information about the sensitized person to himself can be somewhat embarrassing for him. He is a comparatively private person and can resent people treating his personal emotions as percentages of a series of traits on a chart. Consequently, although the information should be delivered to him, it needs to be conveyed in a personal, private and confidential manner. It should also be understood that the information about him is confidential and treated with professional respect. After his initial sensitivities have subsided, he will probably be fascinated with the process and somewhat surprised at how well that the firm understands him. He will generally be impressed the firm took the time necessary to understand him. He will interpret this as a desire to know and work with him as an individual. This will be especially flattering to him, and he will appreciate the lengths the firm has obviously gone through to ensure a proper fit between himself and the operational needs of the organization.

The sensitized person will be interested to hear that certain processes are in place for the orderly transaction of business. As for the performance appraisal, he will want to hear that performance is the bottom line on the final evaluation. He knows that he can be a bit socially awkward. Knowing real results are what matter most will reassure him that he is making the right choice. Remember, the sensitized person is basically emotionally insecure and wants some reassurance that he will be rated (for promotions, advancement, bonus, etc.) on some objective criteria that is largely independent of his interpersonal social style.

Often the sensitized person is highly creative and is aware of this trait. Like most creative people, he is happy to abide by the rules, regulations, and policies of the company. However, he may also feel the need to show his self-perceived independence in some way. This could be expressed by simply reading the newspaper for the first ten minutes of the workday morning. It can mean occasionally wearing different colored socks, or taking a two-hour lunch once a month. If these behavior infringements are not too upsetting to the company rules, then he should be allowed to indulge himself—as long as he is creative and is making a solid contribution to the company.

By comparison, some people are immature, and although aspiring to be creative and insightful, generally are not. The difference between these two types of people is usually fairly easy to determine. The appropriate management correction of the behavior is readily available. In the same way, the sensitized person needs to be told about the hierarchy of the firm and where he fits in. He is less concerned about his advancement, but he needs to be informed about the proper respect for his superiors in the organization.

AGGRESSIVE

The candidate typified by the aggressive behavior style is frequently successful in a marketing-oriented professional services firm. This person is most successful when the trait is combined with other traits, especially that of the overachiever, entrepreneur, or active. The aggressive person is dynamic, at times forceful, and persevering. He can be socially overbearing but generally controls this tendency and channels his energies into productive efforts. Many senior executives of professional service and other corporations have a significant amount of the aggressive trait. They see problems as challenges. Accordingly, they marshal their emotional, mental, and work experience skills to meet problems and improve their own lot along the way. Consistent with this picture, when sufficiently controlled, the aggressive person is frequently charismatic and a natural leader.

It may be surprising, but the aggressive person will be interested in and impressed with someone who knows the history of the firm. The reason for this is that he is a reader of historical biographies and believes in studying the past as a prologue to the future. He sees history and tradition (as well as pomp, circumstance, and ritual) as an important part of the management process. Moreover, he will be impressed that the firm, too, shares this belief in the importance of knowing and sharing a history of the corporate roots.

He will be very interested in his initial job duties and especially concerned about the breadth of his authority. He will in time press these limits, wherever they are set. He wants to know the people reporting to him so that he can effectively build his team. He will also be interested in his superiors. The information he learns about them will help him to understand who may be in a position to block his initiatives. He is somewhat suspicious of others' motives and assumes that other influential people are driven by the same desire for control that flourishes in his mind.

The aggressive person, like the sensitized person, is driven by emotional insecurity. Certain phrases are applicable to the aggressive person, like "the firm needs his dynamic sense of accomplishment, but he has to be sure not to overstep the limits of his authority." Or, he can be described as a "can-do person, who needs the cooperation of others to reach his full potential." Provide him the credit he is due, but remind him of the necessity to practice self-discipline. He will be receptive to the feedback and will probably be interested in hearing about ways to motivate (and control) his subordinates because he is frequently concerned about social control.

The candidate who is personified by the aggressive behavior style is also interested in the internal mechanics of the firm. He will show a keen interest in criteria for performance appraisal and advancement. At the same time, he is more than willing to do the work necessary to get ahead, but he will be eager to hear an objective accounting of his results. He tends to over-inflate his accomplishments and sees his contribution to many group efforts as larger than others on the team. He is not too unfair in this assessment, but he is somewhat biased and strong-willed in pointing out his contribution.

The structure of the organization is important to the aggressive candidate in similar ways as to the entrepreneur. He is inclined to see value in hobnobbing with senior-level personnel. He sees himself as part of the power elite of the organization. He will want to be aware of who the real power brokers are so that he can work at impressing them in social and business situations. Interestingly, senior-level personnel will be evenly divided on the value of such behavior. They will either find this behavior quite positive and encourage it, or they will see it as an obvious nuisance. The result is that the aggressive person will become increasingly selective about who he chooses to target and befriend.

COMPULSIVE

The person who is primarily compulsive is statistically unusual in Western society. The person, when identified, takes on many of the outward behavior characteristics of the movie character Mr. Spock from the *Star Trek* series. He is essentially so logical, rational, objective, and thorough in his task completion that he appears to lack much emotional verve or effect. He can appear cold and unemotional in his seemingly mechanistic demeanor. However, once people come to know and understand his particular manner of interaction, he can be incredibly likeable and very well meaning.

Again, it is rare to find a person with this dominant behavior. It is much more common to see the trait combined with, and dominated by, the aggressive trait. The aggressive-compulsive person can and will be a successful marketing-oriented professional. However, when the compulsive person does arrive on the professional scene, it is wise to be prepared to deal with his perceptions of "the" important matters.

Typically, the compulsive person is less interested in the subject matter per se. He is focused on the method being used to present the material to him. He finds many topics worth studying. It should be emphasized that he is most impressed with the thoroughness of the manner in which the topics are delivered. The prime exception to this rule is the description of his job duties. He will be very interested in learning about the exact nature, definition, and scope of his responsibilities. Once he accepts the mandate to perform his job function, he can operate like a train crossing the prairies of Kansas. He thinks, functions, and delivers with a simple and almost unalterable straight-line logic.

He will find the interpretation of his temperament intellectually amusing. He will probably be more interested in the construction of the instruments that defined it than in the actual results. He may show some natural curiosity about the results, but his main concern will be with the logic and validity of the questionnaires used to determine his behavior style.

Once he moves beyond this level of analysis, he will be glad to hear that his sense of logic and rationality are needed in the firm. However, he will not be unduly swayed by the firm's need for his services. These comments should be included but not overemphasized. The need for his type of thinking is obvious to him and, although not the least arrogant about it, he thinks others should readily recognize this. Further, he will not attempt to extract more money from the firm for his special skills. Neither will he be likely to budge from what he considers a reasonable level of compensation for his services. It is the overall logic of the presentation that he hears and that is most impressive to him.

The compulsive person will show a rational level of interest in the performance appraisal system, benefits, and perks that are part of the employment package. He will be most interested in understanding how they work as a mechanical process. He is less interested in projecting himself in the best possible light, or in scoring the most points in terms of a compensation or bonus system. He is motivated to understand the statistical formula behind them.

The same basic intellectual interest will motivate him to learn about the company structure and design. He is not interested in using the information for any Machiavellian intrigue but merely to better understand his place in the organization and how his function contributes to the overall environment. The compulsive person is not ego-less and certainly has some interest in achieving a position of importance, recognition, and income potential. However, like most engineers, he goes about the process of improving his lot within the organization by a strict adherence to some formal rules of logic. He would be very uncomfortable achieving his goals any other way.

Chapter Six

TRAINING: PROCESS AND PRESENTATION

Training is defined as the process of teaching the selected professional personnel how to improve and develop their skills and abilities. It is management's responsibility to form the selected personnel into a successful team. This is not an easy task, and not every manager can teach every capable person. The more defined the skill level of the incoming new professionals, the more effective the manager will be in training them in the skills necessary to be successful in the firm.

This training function really has two components: training for skills in the area of professional competence and training for skills in the area of marketing professional services. Most professional people coming into the firm have a basic level of knowledge in their technical area. This entry level can often be expanded in formal and informal workshops and skill-building training programs. The type of training activity designed to improve technical knowledge is beyond the scope of this text. Just as most professional personnel are adequately trained in their area of technical expertise, many are not well trained in the area of marketing themselves, their products or professional services. The marketing of the person, and his products and services, is the focus of this section.

The recruiting captain and the professional service firm have invested a significant amount of time, money, and energy into the selection, assessment, and enlistment of the new professional person. The person is no longer another candidate. He has accepted a position at one of the six levels introduced in Chapter 1 and is now a member of the firm. What next? Given the nature and very definition of a marketing-oriented professional service firm, the sales process is an important part of his introduction to and initial training within the firm. In fact, the overall effectiveness of the training that the new person receives will influence his productivity for some time to come. The indoctrination can largely determine if the time, money, and energy spent on the person to that point will be a reasonable investment or a misuse of company funds.

The recruiting captain usually assumes that he has hired a winner. If a team selection process has been used, then other members of the interviewing group and members of the firm should be inclined to feel the same way. However, the recruiting captain is the most enthusiastic about his new hire. He may feel that he has enlisted an experienced professional person (despite his level in the organization), who needs little or no coaching or training. Generally speaking, this is one of the most frequent and egregious assumptions that managers make about their new hires.

Professional personnel, even those joining a marketing-oriented firm, are people who are at least to a certain extent sales mongers. As such, they are subject to all sorts of aspirations and perceptions that will influence their job performance. They are better not thought of as pawns in a chess match, or as soldiers to be sent to the front line in order to shore up existing weakness in a given area—unless there is some prior consultation. They probably possess a considerable amount of knowledge, technical ability, and interpersonal skill. Depending on their behavior style, they want/need a combination of security, status, recognition, information, and encouragement.

The more experienced sales-oriented professional service people will have the strongest faith in themselves. They are productive in technical and sales areas, and they believe that they are the key ingredient in their own history of success. Certainly they are interested in working with and for their new leaders. They joined the firm, in part, because they saw that the social environment would reward some of their basic needs. Other capable personnel will be less sure of their individual talents and be more willing to admit to the value of a strong team-orientation, and the reality that in a large-scale project more than enough credit is available for each contributing team member.

New personnel with a variety of behavior styles will have to admit some dependence on their supervisors for technical support and motivation in the sales process. It is the new person's manager who ultimately provides him or her with the equipment to be successful in the firm. He may accomplish this by providing technical input or, alternatively, by running interference with *his* boss until the new person has established a foothold in an area of the business. However, whether it is widely recognized or not, the manager almost universally plays a significant role in the success of any new person. The manager who thinks first and foremost of his people and how best to develop them will frequently develop the strongest base of support both among immediate reports and also within the entire organization.

PROCESS

The new professional can be thought of as a precious commodity, and he needs to be treated as a unique person. His talents, skills, and abilities represent a marketing opportunity for the firm to capitalize on. In most cases, he needs to be developed in order for him and the firm to take full advantage of his talents. The new person has been influenced by a host of factors, including parents, teachers, peers, and previous employers. He has developed a certain behavior style that will enable him to be effective in the marketplace. He should be made aware of his behavior style and the inherent pluses and possible developmental needs that it includes. In essence, he needs to be trained in the firm's manner of business in order to reach his own potential.

Many new professionals join a firm after jumping a series of self-described hurdles. They have been interviewed, tested, evaluated, and screened. At a higher level, they have been wined and dined. They may have had expensive seats at a sports event, a night of theater, and even first-class air or private limousine travel. They may well have "bought" the image that firm was sending them during the recruiting process and actually believe they are as good as the firm evidently believes them to be. In some cases the reality of that first Monday morning in the office can be a rude awakening. Naturally, the honeymoon period of employment cannot last forever, but the recent hire should not be suddenly dropped off the face of civility and told to "start producing" the minute he walks in the door. He does need some consideration and facilitation to adjust to the job and the new environment.

This initial indoctrination period should be established on some form of mutual understanding and trust that will last over time. The indoctrination period is brief but serves as a transition from the madcap sense of desire that can surround the recruitment phase to the occasional drudgery that is part of the world of providing professional services. This process should be a positive one. The new hire should be politely welcomed to his new work environment, introduced to his working peers, given a detailed scope of his duties and expectations, and generally prepared for the training (formal or not) that is to follow.

The professional service person who demonstrates a high degree of either the entrepreneur or aggressive traits may resist formal sales training. He tends to think that he is already aware of most sales techniques and that training is largely a waste of time. Individuals who are marked by behavior patterns of the sensitized and passive traits may feel that they are not likely to be especially effective in a sales role and therefore ask, "Why should they bother with formal training?" The overachievers and active individuals will accept the need for training. The overachiever will because it represents an opportunity to learn; the active will because he enjoys almost any opportunity to interact with others.

Finally, the compulsive person will accept the need for training as a matter of fact, although he may "logically" point out that he is not the best-suited person to receive the training. All the members of the professional staff need to learn that some form of sales training *is* for everyone. Sales is not a four-letter word (it's a five-letter word). This means that everyone should understand and accept that sales, new business, and marketing are the lifeblood of the firm. The importance of sales, and a passing understanding of the basic building blocks of the sales process, should be required of everyone.

By analogy, it is recognized that everyone in the U.S. military is trained in the techniques of basic combat. They may later receive additional training in mechanics, administration, finance, or hundreds of other specialized topics. But everyone receives basic combat training—the process of holding, firing, and cleaning a weapon—because the basic function of any military force is to be prepared for combat. In the same way, the basic function of any professional service firm is to provide a service to clients. Ultimately, this service includes a sales component.

In order to reach his full potential, the new person must respect the company, its products and services, its marketing philosophy, and its approach to working with clients. Typically, of most importance is the relationship the professional person has with his sales superior. The person should be convinced of his manager's interest in him and his manager's desire and drive to help him to become successful. The person will listen to a manager who has done it successfully himself. He must admire the skill set of the manager (although he does not have to emulate it) and his ability to effectively sell business for the firm.

The new professional person and the manager do not necessarily have to form a relationship of personal interest, but the new person must respect the sales ability of his boss. Some of the most likeable bosses demonstrate an active-passive behavior style. This means that they are warm, personable, likeable, and well intentioned. They readily commiserate with their subordinates, and quickly communicate an understanding of the frustrations of the sales process. Unfortunately, these people frequently *do not* make for successful superiors when they are required to lead a sales effort. They are simply too soft emotionally. They are neither sufficiently disciplined, competitive, nor aggressive to be successful in a sales leadership role.

By contrast, the active-aggressive supervisor and the overachiever-entrepreneur supervisor are less likely to be considered great interpersonal friends by their subordinates, but they often are the most successful sales leaders. They are well respected by their subordinates to a certain extent because they lead by example and force the new professional person to the point of sale. At this juncture, they insist on well-planned and persuasive sales presentations.

The active-aggressive manager is personable, well meaning, and interpersonally engaging. He is also dynamic, driven, and socially aggressive. He can be forceful, but he is not autocratic without good reason. He would never require a subordinate to do anything in the sales process that he has not already done many times himself. In some ways, the active-aggressive manager can be compared to an outspoken, control-oriented but highly successful athletic coach. In his own way, he is highly charismatic and inspirational, and he achieves positive results from his subordinates because they follow his instructions. He may not realize his potential, but he manages his staff to achieve a level of success. Sometimes this level is beyond what could rationally be expected of the talent level of the people on his team. His motto is composed of two undeniable, irrevocable ideas, and he frequently repeats them in a myriad of different ways. They were first used by the real-life and legendary Coach Vince Lombardi. They are: "Believe in me," and "Do as I say."

The overachiever-entrepreneur manager also achieves positive results with his subordinates. He attains his goals with a slightly different emphasis. He is a highly self-disciplined person who is eager to achieve a position of importance, monetary wealth, and social status within the corporate hierarchy. Frequently he is socially polished to the point of being considered "smooth" and gracious. At the same time he is highly competitive, driven, and goal directed. Such managers resemble the fictional hero James Bond. They read people (subordinates, peers, and clients) with equal ease and are very adroit in communicating a sense of professional concern that is directed at each member of the audience. They are persuasive and convincing sales personnel.

The overachiever-entrepreneur manager consciously recruits personnel in his own image and entices his subordinates to work harder and smarter in order to achieve the "good life"—a life style that the manager readily demonstrates. These managers achieve their goals by recruiting and training a small cadre of professional service "commandos" who are devoted to the manager and aspire to walk in his footsteps. In turn, the manager is dedicated to his most productive people, who sometimes reach positions of influence, power, and monetary success. These managers function as role models for new recruits.

Both the active-aggressive and overachiever-entrepreneur managers demonstrate a definable form of social and interpersonal charisma that is effective with the types of people they recruit. They mold the new professional people into a formidable unit and achieve success with them. These types of managers are leaders and have proven records of success. They teach and reinforce that whatever "selling skills" the new professional has been taught in the classroom are applicable to the field. They consciously build on what the person knows or believes and shape his behavior pattern into one that can effectively market professional services.[1]

SALES KNOWLEDGE REQUIREMENT

The new professional person comes to the firm with an education, some training, and work experience that is at least technically applicable to the task at hand. However, there is almost always a gap of some size between what the new person already knows and what he has to learn in order to be effective with the new company, and this is true at all levels in the firm. The person is new to the firm and probably new to the products as well. He needs to be become aware of his specific role in the sales process and with respect to his clients and co-workers. He needs to understand the functions he is expected to perform and the environment in which he will be working. In general, the new person must gain some knowledge of the company in four areas: products and services, business environment, history and policies, and operations and procedures.

Products and Services. It is often surprising to many *new* professional service personnel that they know more about the firm's products and services than the clients do. However, the fear of not knowing something that a client may ask about will spur the person to study and thoroughly understand the firm's portfolio of products and services. At a minimum, he should be aware of every product that *he* is representing. Naturally he needs to be aware of the firm's other products, but he needs to know his own especially well. He should be drilled on why the product has the given features it does and what advantages and benefits the product potentially has for the client. The new professional person should also be prepared to discuss the product's limitations and possible failures. He should have a rough idea about pricing, but on this issue he should defer to more experienced staff. Alternatively, he can cite the need to check with the home office or prepare a proposal, including cost estimates, for a given product or service.

Business Environment. The professional person should be aware of his competitors. He is not interested in dragging down the qualifications or abilities of these people, but he certainly is aware of their products, services, and methods of operation. He must understand the competitive advantages of other products, and, although professional services are seldom bought on the basis of price alone, this is a factor that will be especially considered in recessionary times. He should know the type of success the competitors are having in the marketplace and have some understanding of why.

The next set of business (environmental) conditions that the new person must understand are the easiest to state but the hardest to learn. The professional needs to learn the client's existing needs and whether they are currently being satisfied by some other service firm. Almost all professionals can improve their ability in this area, although some people seem to have a more natural talent for acquiring these skills, principally, the overachiever, entrepreneur, active, and aggressive. While they demonstrate the most natural ability for learning these skills, every professional should be encouraged to improve in this area.

New employees also need to understand the both overt and subtle influences that force clients to change, including changing socio-economic lifestyles, national pressures, technological advances, regulatory influences, and the general business environment. They also need to understand the subtle pressures that move the client toward him or another provider of professional services. Finally, to the extent possible, they should steer the client toward making the best possible decision.

History and Policies. A thorough knowledge of the company's history and an understanding of the philosophy behind its policies will enable the new person to successfully represent the company. In essence, he needs to be grounded in the tradition of why the company acts the way it does, what policies and general rules the company is especially proud of, and which aspects of the company can be used repeatedly as part of a marketing campaign or in an individual sales presentation. He should also be able to defend any policy that runs contrary to the industry trend and make a reasonable case about why the company implemented and maintains the policy. He does not necessarily have to agree with the policy, but he should be able to provide a rational explanation for it.

Operations and Procedures. This is an important segment of the professional person's identity as he markets the firm's products. He should be able to discuss the other critical departments in the organization, as well as the overall administrative and research functions. It is vital to be aware of any client satisfaction measures that the company uses, and the professional should readily endorse the client's use of these "hot lines" to inform senior management of any problems resulting from his oversights. He should not be afraid to lay out the company structure and defend it as a generally sound, but ultimately reasonable, approach to doing business.

SALES SKILL REQUIREMENT

Once the new professional person has learned the basic information about the firm and its products, services, environment, and approach, then he is ready to develop his sales skills. Knowledge can be gained by reading a book at night by oneself. Skills, and in particular sales skills, require practice. Much like the secret to owning successful property is location, so a significant part of developing successful selling skills is practice. This means being with clients or in realistic yet simulated conditions.

Learning sales skills can be compared to learning an athletic skill. The more natural talent a person possesses, the better he will perform. However, the practice of an athletic routine does significantly improve almost anyone's performance. In the same way, practice selling (with appropriate coaching) will almost certainly improve performance. Thus, the professional person's manager should have sales experience and habits that have been proven successful. The person who enjoys participation in an athletic event "for the fun of it," will practice as long as he is enjoying himself. Similarly, the professional person will practice his sales skills as long as he feels he is learning some valuable skills. The key is to impress upon the new professional person that sales is everybody's business and that it is an integral part of his job function.

Many less experienced professional people do not readily understand the need for sales activity and the absolute necessity of cultivating new accounts. However, once they are informed of the reality of life in a professional service firm, they are more willing to adopt a proactive approach to selling the firm's products and services. This understanding will not, however, readily enable them to deal with rejection of their sales presentations. This will be frustrating, demeaning, and in some cases embarrassing for them. They may begin to see themselves as less professional because they are required to sell and also act in a professional advice-giving mode.

This is a problem that every manager must face in developing new professional people. In essence, the manager must understand that whatever sales ability the professional person lacks, the manager must compensate for. So managers should be encouraged to select personnel who demonstrate at least some sales ability. Short of identifying the personnel who obviously possess the traits necessary to be successful in sales, the manager should focus heavily on the degree to which the new person demonstrates the overachiever trait. In sufficient amounts, this trait will enable the new professional person who is not naturally talented in the sales area to be much more effective than might otherwise have been thought possible. If the person is sufficiently self-disciplined, he will force himself to take on certain sales responsibilities and will perform in an effective manner.

A high degree of the overachiever trait will increase the likelihood of success. However, other structural variables can also facilitate the pattern of success. The sales training sequence should be designed to maximize the professional person's positive experiences. Initially, he should accompany other professionals on sales calls, where his function is to observe, take notes, and politely blend into the atmosphere. Following the sales call, he is included in any debriefing, but he is not expected to make presentations for some time. The purpose of these observation calls is to avoid an early knockout punch to the new professional's ego, causing him to decide that professional services is not his preferred work environment.

The new person must learn to apply some basic selling techniques. These methods can be learned in one of many selling courses. The value of participating in at least one such basic course is that the professional person (who may have no exposure or training in sales per se) will be exposed to and should learn an outline of the sales process. Sales is no more magical than learning any other skill, and many basic courses provide an outline that includes some valuable tools to apply in the sales process.

In time, the professional person must learn to develop an instinct for a selling opportunity. He must be able to perceive and understand the client's potential problematic issues. He will have to develop a sense of polite probing to discover facts that will enable him to bring client needs to the surface and then provide a valid solution to the problems that exist. A whole variety of skills will have to be developed. It will not be easy, and the process will require time. One of the most important generic skills is the ability to listen effectively, understand, and react appropriately when clients are directly expressing their needs. Perhaps the most critical aspect of the professional's learning curve is self-criticism. The professional person must be able to learn from his experiences.

The best training method is selling itself. The more resourceful people will learn sales skills early in their career. However, the process cannot be forced. Only a small part of the necessary sales methods can be learned by reading and contemplating the process. In preparation for "live" sales presentations, casework, role plays, artificial games, and pretend sessions can be used. Sales calls can be rehearsed in one's head, but until they are played out in front of an audience, little actual learning will take place. The new person must watch the experienced professional and see what he has been taught in the classroom result in increased sales. The new person has to see the experienced professional plan, propose, discuss, and close a deal successfully. He has to see and experience all the steps of the sales process. He has to interact with real people, experience live risk, and celebrate victory or plan the next approach. Perhaps most importantly, he has to learn from each experience. For this reason, the field training has to be complemented by information and techniques taught in the class-room. The field has to be an extension of the practice sessions with the field training the most critical aspect of the process.

The experienced professional readily understands the necessity for a coaching session after each presentation. The material covered should be outlined in advance and reviewed in a systematic fashion. It is not an opportunity to laugh over a clever remark, or to comment on the impossibility of meeting a certain client's demands. This should be a disciplined and detailed review of the meeting from a sales perspective. The experienced person should describe how what he did or said relates to material covered in the classroom. He should note critical or atypical incidents to highlight certain behaviors or methods that can be used. He should specifically explain which events in the course of the meeting went right and which events detoured. This is not a fault-finding session but an opportunity to objectively discuss a meeting from a learning perspective and to initially prepare for the next presentation.

Once the new person has sat through enough meetings, held the flip chart, and provided some ancillary information in a meeting, it will be his turn to actually propose a meeting agenda and head the client presentation. In this case, the roles are reversed. During a meeting the experienced professional will be taking notes, nodding appropriately, and contributing a tactical "yes, I see" at the right time. Again, this presentation will be followed by an in-depth review of the presentation and the experienced professional will provide feedback to the new person. In these situations some experienced professionals are better at providing feedback than others. It may be somewhat surprising that the entrepreneur and aggressive behavior types are typically the least patient in providing the kind of insightful and detailed information that is most needed for improvement. These people will candidly say they do not have time to teach "everybody everything." They will purposely seek out individuals like themselves who possess a more competitive, impatient, and risk-prone behavior style. Such people are well matched to the entrepreneur and aggressive managers because they are less likely to readily accept criticism.

In contrast, the active-passive manager is often the most considerate and insightful. He takes the time to offer corrections and suggestions to new professional personnel in learning to sell services. These managers are perceptive, compassionate, and genuinely concerned about building a team approach to selling. Hence, they will make themselves available to teach others. They project a selling style that is effective, but they can lack the instinct to go for a close, which their entrepreneur and aggressive peers may have.

This method of joint client-calls can be expensive. It requires the time of the new and experienced professional. However, it is the best way to ensure that the new person learns the process. The new person may be reluctant to "perform" in front of the more experienced person—he is afraid of performing poorly and anticipates being the subject of harsh criticism. However, this sense of anxiety should also spur the new person to be prepared and to diligently follow whatever script he has been given. The supervisory review should emphasize the positive aspects of the new person's presentation.

Countless studies point out that more learning takes place with positive rather than negative reinforcement. The experience should be seen as positive by the person, even if many corrections have to be made. If the new person continuously fails to modify his behavior or to show signs of responding to the experienced person's comments, then this should be addressed as an attitude issue. However, whenever possible the new person should be given positive reinforcement in a developmental fashion.

Most sales training programs are little more than a road map that the new professional will either use or not, depending on his perception of the usefulness of the map. Some people will study the map assiduously and seldom, if ever, deviate from its planned route. They will see it as the answer to their needs. Typically, these people will show a large portion of the passive trait in their behavior style. They will abide by the rules and carefully follow any instructions, but they will seldom achieve spectacular results. They will, at best, approach their sales quota but seldom actually attain or surpass it. These same people may be inclined to "blame" the map, or the sales training program, if they are not successful in arriving on time at their sales quota.

Other people will see the sales training map as a useful overall guideline, but only that. They tend to improvise and adapt the sales methods being taught to their own behavior style and perceptions. Typically, these people show behavior styles of the entrepreneur or aggressive. If these people achieve success, they are inclined to credit primarily themselves, with some backhanded reference to the initial training they may have received. If not successful, these same people are the most likely to blame the economy, the home office, or lack of any really good training. With reference to the training, they will indicate that it was fine as far as it went, but it just did not cover enough of the basics and left the bulk of the learning up to them. They could only acquire learning through direct experience, and since the economy (or whatever other outside source) was so bad, they could not achieve any real success in the sales process.

The person characterized by the active behavior style will generally endorse the rules and methods presented in the training program and will try to follow them in his presentations. However, he is so naturally energetic that he can become easily sidetracked and follow an alternative method that is perhaps, surprisingly, equally successful. If prompted, he will readily endorse the training methods prescribed by the company and will try to teach them to others. However, he will also include a significant portion of individual interpretation of the guidelines provided in the manual.

The key to maximizing the performance of individuals with each of these behavior types is to measure the degree to which each possesses the overachiever trait. To the extent that they possess sufficient discipline, they can be allowed to function independently. However, most people, even with a reasonable amount of the overachiever trait, will need supervision to be fully successful in any sales training program. Supervision of some kind is required to ensure that the individuals do not deviate too far from the material in the sales training program.

An efficient way to do this is to develop a highly standardized plan and to ensure that the people who use it and supervise it possess a high degree of the overachiever behavior style. Without this trait, the plan will be interpreted and modified according to the whims of those using and supervising it. For example, the entrepreneur is a highly competitive individual who sees himself operating as a lone wolf. He likes to achieve *his* goals *his* way, and because of his self-defined importance and need for independence, he may resent having to follow a set program.

The active person can be something of an exhibitionist at heart. He is likely to improvise and increase his personal involvement with the presentation and with the client personally. He likes to be friendly and personable, so he may be inclined to overplay his special role in the presentation, albeit in a thoroughly friendly and personable manner. He will tend to draw himself to center stage and talk when perhaps he should be listening.

The aggressive person is sometimes highly control oriented. He may be inclined to push too soon for the close, when the client is still in a deciding mode. The aggressive person has an inherent dislike for ambiguity and plans ad infinitum to eliminate any possible escape from his sales presentation. He will not easily take "no" for an answer, and he is eager to get to "yes," sometimes before the client is ready to commit to any answer. Although people who demonstrate these three behavior styles—entrepreneur, active, and aggressive—are in many ways very capable sales personnel, they need to also show a high degree of the overachiever, or to be effectively controlled by their supervisors or the environment. When used consistently, the standardization will benefit everyone, including the new professional person, the experienced person who is beginning to expand his sales responsibilities for the first time, and the organization as a whole. This standardization is designed to be used as a track, with established boundaries for the professional person to tread. Some people will find it restrictive and may rebel against it. However, if properly drawn and explained, no one should find it overly restrictive, and if the overall company benefits from such a program, it will be to the advantage of all who use it.

Most professional people, even those experienced in sales, prefer having at least an outline to use as a guideline when making a presentation. In some ways, not having this aid is like going into a meeting without an agenda. It can be done successfully, but most clients and consultants feel better prepared and more at ease when they can share an outline at the beginning of the meeting. In the same way, if the professional person has a sales outline in his head, he is better prepared to lead a discussion to the point where he wants to go.

CLIENT PRESENTATION

Training is an ongoing process for the professional service person. A good part of that training takes place in front of different clients, explaining and presenting the firm's products and services. The client presentation includes everything that occurs while in front of the client. It is sometimes described as the "message segment" of the meeting. A positive presentation should persuade the client to move forward with the process. It should reinforce the client's perception that he needs to change some existing plan or process in his organization, and the product presented in this meeting may be the vehicle to achieve that end. The presentation should diplomatically help the client to see the need for change *and* motivate him to take the first steps in that process. Ideally, the presentation should anticipate the client's objections, and at least include a segment that will allow the objections to be answered. The presentation should be fact based and well researched. Moreover, it must to be prepared for the individual needs of the client in the room, that is, the vocabulary and style of the material should be geared to the needs and expectations of the audience.

The actual success of a presentation is not always easy to determine, especially in marketing professional services. If a presentation is made and a client agrees on the spot to use the product or service, then the presentation may be considered successful. However, this does not always happen. The client who is apparently very interested may not follow through and actually purchase the product. Conversely, other clients who appear only mildly interested may in time indicate that a given presentation was key in their deciding to move ahead with the proposed project.

How important is the style of presentation? An old but generally established adage concerning this issue goes something like, "The sale is *made* in the first five minutes in front of the prospect, and *lost* in the last five." Can the overall effectiveness of a presentation style or content be touted to be better than others? In some sense yes, depending on the client, the product, and the presentation.

PRESENTATION OBJECTIVES

Some time ago, the primary and perhaps the only purpose of the presentation was to convince the client to buy the product or service. However, this single-purpose approach has changed. The forces that motivated this change are subtle, but they include more sophisticated clients, wiser professionals, and a new marketplace. Information is more transportable now, and clients are insisting on information meetings as a precursor to a sales presentation, and professional consultants are obliging.

Clients expect consultants to candidly inform them about a variety of topics relevant to the marketplace in general and about the details of their particular product. However, increasingly they will not accept the latter without the former. The client wants the professional firm to present its product within a competitive framework, elaborate on the societal effects it may have, and to directly answer ethical considerations about the use and promotion of the product (although research shows that cost alone is frequently a secondary consideration when purchasing professional services). The professional service firm also has some expectations about the presentation. The presentation material and style should facilitate the growth and development of the consultant providing the information, while inspiring the client to positive actions. Thus, the format and style of the presentation will influence the effectiveness of the presenter.

The author conducted a research project on this subject using a number of firms of varying sizes and offering different products and services in a range of unique markets. The research focused on satisfying the needs of the clients, who were the audience during the presentation, and the consultants who presented the material. The objectives were twofold. Client objectives included:

1. Optimal use of time
2. Ethical and complete content
3. Accurate and knowledgeable
4. Match company needs
5. Anticipate objections

The professional service firm objectives concerning a presentation included:

6. Persuade client
7. Increase consultant's acceptance
8. Increase firm's credibility
9. Assist in consultant supervision
10. Assist in consultant training

A continuous debate exists over which presentation method is most effective for certain products, clients, and consultants. Many people believe that the method that works for them should therefore be used by everybody. Many people can recite famous stories within their industry when the outline for a significant proposal was drawn on and presented from a napkin at a lunch counter. Others can tell about multi-media, many-colored, simulcast presentations that were months in planning, expensive to produce, and complete failures in terms of additional business. Both extremes are memorable precisely because they are so rare. Most of the time, a presentation style can be configured that is appropriate for the meeting place, time, and audience.

The single differentiating characteristic among presentations is its *structure*. A presentation should not be considered "canned" or "not canned." Neither should it be perceived as "structured" or "not structured." These two examples present bipolar differences on a continuum with many intervening degrees between them. For the sake of the research conducted, it was decided to use a five step continuum ranging from completely structured to completely unstructured. These points were defined as follows:

1. *Completely Structured.* The use of technology dominated the sales presentation. Movies, slide shows (some with coordinated sound), video (some computer based) and even film strips were used as the predominant means of explaining the product/service. The consultant was largely relegated to the function of technology set-up person and secondarily to answer simple questions not covered by presentation.

2. *Partially Structured.* The consultant leans heavily on prepared material. He flips through a book (often with color graphs and charts), uses a prepared flip chart, or relies on pre-printed brochures. The function of the consultant is to explain, from looking at the prepared material, how a given product/service can increase the client's efficiency, and so forth.

3. *Quasi Structured.* The consultant delivers an obviously memorized speech. He presents the material in a direct and somewhat parrot-like fashion. If interrupted, he can lose his concentration and be forced to repeat a portion of the material in order to remember his place in the delivery sequence. In this scenario, visual aids may or may not be used.

4. *Non-structured.* The consultant is allowed complete flexibility, primarily in the area of wording. He delivers his message in a way that he decides is optimal for the situation. He follows a general outline and may speak from a single-sheet discussion outline, but he appears to be more spontaneous. Again, visual aids are optimal, but, if utilized, they play a secondary role to the interpersonal and presentation skills of the consultant.

5. *Completely Unstructured.* The consultant is literally free to describe the product/service. He may describe the material in any way that he sees best. He is independent and not required to follow any set script or outline. For the most part, the consultant varies his approach for each client setting and might describe his approach as customized to the needs of the client as he sees them.

It probably comes as no surprise that most professional firms use a combination of two or even three presentation styles. However, the higher a person progresses in the firm, the more likely he is to use *styles four or five*. Less experienced professional personnel are much more likely to use highly structured presentation styles. More experienced, higher level, and more successful professional people will use the less structured presentation styles.

In terms of the person's behavior style and preferred presentation style, the higher the passive and/or sensitized traits in the person, the more likely he or she is to use the structured presentation styles. Some sensitized and passive people who have reached senior levels in the firm were "successful" in marketing their products and services. However, it should be noted that these traits were not as common as the entrepreneur, active, and aggressive traits in senior marketing-oriented personnel. The people who are high on the sensitized and passive traits are less sure of their interpersonal presentation skills and are more likely to rely on prepared material to communicate their ideas than to use their own interpersonal skills. When asked about this preference, many of the passive and sensitized people made such comments as:

"Look, the company has gone to a great deal of expense, probably including a fair amount of research about this, and they have prepared these materials. Since the company has prepared them, I feel semi-obligated to use them. Why else did the company invest in them? I am a company person. I believe in following the guidelines. And I am happy to use the material. Besides, it makes it a lot easier to speak from existing material. I don't have to waste a lot of time explaining myself and the terms I use."

In direct contrast to this preference for adopting the ready-made material, the people most likely to *not* use the material are those whose behavior patterns included a high degree of the entrepreneur, active, and aggressive traits. At the lower levels of the professional firm, people with these traits resisted using the structured approach more than people with other behavior trait patterns, although they generally used the material because they were told to do so. At the higher levels of the organization, these people resisted and did not use the structured approach. They saw themselves as too independent, original, and clever to use the prepared material. Comments from these people included the following:

"Don't get me wrong, that stuff from the home office is good as far as it goes, but it is just too confining for my clients. I know my clients, and they know me. We know what to expect from each other. If I brought out some canned looking material, they would begin to think that I had lost it. Again, don't get me wrong. The material is good as far at it goes, but I have to use it as a base and then go beyond what they say is good. Finally, I get my results. I invoice my quota of sales hours every month, and so they leave me alone."

It is interesting to note the response of the managers to the material with respect to their subordinates. The managers with the more aggressive behavior styles were the most insistent that their subordinates at the lower levels use the more structured approaches, although they, at the higher levels, refused to use the structured approach. When queried about this apparently inconsistent practice, these managers suggested that they wanted to be sure that the lower-level people followed a consistent pattern. They suspected that the "better" fellow aggressive-type professionals at the lower ranks would resent it, but then they could change once they passed through this phase of their training.

By comparison, the entrepreneur managers indicated that they "couldn't care less what presentation style their underlings used . . . as long as they brought in the business." Finally, the managers who were typified by the active behavior style felt they should suggest that their subordinates use the prescribed structured methods, but that they would not insist on it. A typical comment from one such manager was, "In all honesty, I can't make them follow some rule that I ignored when I was in that position. Besides a 'canned' presentation doesn't fit people like them (people with active behavior styles). Besides, it really is only a guideline, not a firm rule."

The ten objectives listed earlier, equally divided into issues that are important to the client and the service firm, along with the five-point rating scale of the degree of structure in the presentation, were given to a number of professional service firm executives (ranked at organization levels four, five, and six as defined in Chapter 1). These executives were experienced in buying and marketing professional services. They were considered excellent judges of what is important to potential clients, since they purchased professional services from other firms. The others were considered knowledgeable about what is important in developing professional service personnel, since they held positions as senior-level marketing officers in professional service firms. Their ratings for the ten objectives are listed in Table 6.1.

The contents of this table provide some useful insights into how to best approach some clients with specific presentation styles. Of course, these generalizations cannot be applied to every situation, but they are insightful and can serve as starting points for further discussion and experimentation.

Figure 6.1
Ratings for Client (1-5) and Professional Service Firm (6-10): Objectives during Marketing Presentation

	Completeley Structured	Partially Structured	Quasi Structured	Non Structured	Completely Unstructured
1. Optimal use of time	3.2	3.3	2.1	4.2	2.1
2. Complete content	4.1	4.3	3.3	3.1	2.8
3. Accurate and knowledgeable	4.8	4.2	1.5	3.1	1.7
4. Match company needs	3.1	3.4	2.7	4.1	4.4
5. Anticipate objections	3.2	4.0	1.9	4.5	3.2
6. Persuade client	1.5	2.3	1.7	4.3	3.9
7. Increase consultant's acceptance	2.1	3.2	2.2	4.4	3.9
8. Increase firm's credibility	1.2	1.9	3.1	4.5	4.1
9. Assistant in consultant supervision	3.1	4.2	3.2	4.4	1.2
10. Assist in consultant training	4.3	4.2	1.5	4.8	1.6

Each professional person has to use the methods that are most effective for him or her in the situation at hand, but to ignore even these general research findings, is to face the possibility that the professional person is not taking the best approach for a given presentation.

If the presentation is using the client's time in an optimal fashion (objective 1), then the unstructured approach receives the highest rating. The unstructured approach is seen as having sufficient flexibility and adaptability built into it, so that the presenter can slow or speed the presentation to fit the implied or stated needs of the audience. However, the more highly structured approaches also score high in this objective, and this implies that either the audience wants an "experienced" person, who knows how to read the audience and react with appropriate behavior, or the audience prefers a machine that will have a definite time frame to provide its information.

In terms of telling a complete, accurate, and knowledgeable story (objectives 2 and 3), the more structured approaches score the highest rankings. Again, the audience seems to indicate that it trusts a fully automated presentation, one that is presumably prepared by a home office committee that is not likely to deliberately risk providing false or misleading information. This does not imply that the audience does not trust the professional person, but the comparatively low scores for the completely unstructured approach suggest that these types of presentations may appear to be more impulsive than factual. Hence the audience is less likely to fully accept everything these unstructured presentations include.

When the need arises to tell the same story repeatedly, the highly structured approach is probably the best alternative. These situations probably occur most often when the alternatives are very simple, the material can be fully explained, and a decision to purchase or not is made following the one presentation. However, if interruptions, questions, and digressions are a part of the presentation, then these structured methods will prove frustrating to both the audience and the presenter.

If the main purpose of the presentation is to meet the stated or implied needs of the company, to anticipate objections, and generally persuade the client to the presenter's way of thinking (objectives 4 and 5), then the less structured methods are preferred. This suggests that when the experienced professional service person can draw on his own experiences, politely rebut and redirect conversations in the direction of his choosing, and focus the attention of the meeting in a manner that he can more directly control, then he will be more successful.

These numbers, and subsequent interview discussions, suggest that the executives believe that the more experienced professional person should be allowed to use *some* form of structured input (overheads, flip chart, audio-visual, etc.), but he should also then quickly and firmly shift from this prepared presentation form to a more dynamic session. The portion of the presentation that is standardized will provide the initial impression that some home-office involvement and stability is included in the process, and that the person delivering the material possesses the intelligence, discipline, and maturity to think independently and adapt the material to the needs of the client. This notion is reinforced by reviewing the numbers for the partially and quasi-structured presentation styles. It appears that memorized and obviously staged presentations are not nearly so effective.

It is interesting to note further that when the professional person is given the most freedom, he, and the firm he represents, is accepted more and is perceived to be the most credible (objectives 7 and 8). Again, this may result from the fact that the most successful and experienced consultants are likely to present their material using this method. But the association is undeniable. The better consultants depend less on technical props and are perceived to be more credible.

It is not too surprising that the more structured approaches are ranked more effective in training the consultant (objectives 9 and 10), although the unstructured approach is the highest ranked of all the categories. The unstructured approach, one that relies on interaction, reading clients, and showing adaptability and professional responsibility, seems to be the highest-rated category overall. However, the *completely* unstructured approach is almost too good to be true. Perhaps in the hands of an exceptionally experienced, mature, and refined professional person, this method is superior. However, too many professional people believe that they have achieved this status, when that perception is not shared by their audience. The members of the audience prefer some structure and want to see the presenter follow some outline, so that they, too, can monitor and feel that they are involved in a joint discussion. The perception that they are being fed a canned speech, or that they are merely bystanders as someone directs the conversation totally at his whim, is generally not as effective as a more interactive and prepared presentation.

NOTE

1. These ideas are elaborated on in James B. Weitzul, *Sales Force Dynamics: Motives, Management, Money, Marketplace* (Westport, Conn.: Quorum Books, 1993).

Chapter Seven

PERFORMANCE: APPRAISAL AND COMPENSATION

Volumes have been written about performance appraisal and compensation. In most professional firms, each of these topics is an important area and is subject to review and update. However, in order to maintain uniformity, one methodology is generally followed in each area. A performance appraisal rating of X generally means that a certain level of performance has been achieved. An increase in compensation of Y means that a specifiable work goal has been reached. Standard and reliable means are used to measure and define changes in a person's position within the firm. Yet, each system also needs to recognize the human element that is part of the dynamics of the system.

Performance appraisal is the systematic review and evaluation of the professional person's work performance over a set period of time. That performance is then compared to some established performance standard. The final step is the communication of that evaluation to the individual. Ideally, this review session should be motivational, upbeat, and developmental for the individual and the firm. Compensation is a broad topic but generally is a function of the performance appraisal. Most firms combine the performance appraisal with a discussion of compensation.

The exact form of compensation can be an increase in salary, draw, or commission. It may mean an altered or increased package of perks, benefits, or stock options. Several other variations on these basic compensation forms can be used to reward the individual for his or her performance over some period of time. Performance appraisal and compensation are frequently associated with promotion within the firm. A positive review, in most circumstances, eventually leads to a promotion into a managerial position.

This general trend is also valid when discussing professional development in a service organization. The value of defining, communicating, and using valid systems of performance appraisal and compensation is universally recognized. The most effective use of these systems involves recognizing and allowing for the idiosyncratic behavior patterns of the individuals that they are designed to manage. Each of the different behavior types can have a separate perception of the value of these tools. The more successful managers use the tools as instruments and incorporate the needs, wants, and aspirations of the individuals that they supervise into the process. That manager can use these broad-based tools more effectively.

The manager needs to allow for the human element in using these tools to more appropriately guide the people within the organization. After all, in a professional service organization, the people themselves represent the products and services of the organization.

PERFORMANCE APPRAISAL

Performance appraisal in a professional service firm can be one of the most misunderstood processes of the firm. However, if properly constructed and applied, it is a powerful tool to motivate behavior. The appraisal process is part of an overall *system*. It is intended to be an integral part, but only a part, of a total management system. Properly used, it is an influential instrument. The appraisal is most effective when it is a periodic, but regularly scheduled, event. It should be designed to measure and compare recent performance against some form of established and achievable goals. Every professional service firm faces deadlines, pressure situations, and tight work time frames. However, the performance appraisal process is one activity that has to be included with those activities.

It should not be put off or relegated to a quick lunch. Giving such short shrift to this critical activity will only encourage a similarly lackluster attitude among the people receiving such reviews. Certain types of managers are inclined to provide just such appraisals, as will be discussed later. At the same time, the review process cannot be speeded up to fill a temporary void in an otherwise busy schedule. For example, completing a new review within 3 to 4 months of the previous one because the time is temporarily available before the rush of new projects begins sends the wrong message to the subordinates and will ultimately serve a negative value.

The appraisal system should include a reasonable variety of goals, which should be mutually agreed upon by the subordinate and the manager. Otherwise, the subordinate may feel that he has little or no chance of meeting the goals and may not try as hard as he otherwise would to reach them. Goals that are assigned by a boss to a subordinate without some input from the subordinate can destroy motivation. The person being reviewed has to believe that he or she at least participated in establishing the goals to be judged by later.

Studies show that people who participate in the goal-setting process believe that they have an increased chance of meeting them. Some managers do this deliberately, but most often when the subordinate is not included in the goal-setting process, it is merely an oversight on the part of the manager. Curiously, such managers are quite anxious to meet with their manager and to jointly establish their goals for the next review period.

Once the review is completed and certain areas are recognized as needing improvement (and again, these should be jointly decided during the review process), the first part is complete. Next, the manager should show a good deal of skill in counseling and coaching the subordinate about how to improve his or her behavior. This part of the process represents an opportunity for the manager to change certain job-related behavior(s) and motivate the person to change. This cannot be the only time that the manager uses his or her motivational skills with a subordinate, but it is a key opportunity to do just that. This coaching is frequently the bond that unites the manager and subordinate between review periods.

The manager provides specific examples of behavior that needs to be modified and conveys to the subordinate that he has interest in seeing the subordinate change, wants to help him improve, and is professionally committed to assist him. This is not an easy process. To do this effectively requires emotional energy, concern, and insight. Failing to do it properly will lead to either unchanged behavior, indifference, or outright antagonism from the subordinate toward the manager and the firm.

Everyone involved in the performance appraisal process should readily understand that improving the performance of the subordinate has value for the individual, the manager, and the organization as a whole. Some people are highly individualistic in their approach to achieving work goals, and others demonstrate a much stronger team orientation. However, most professional people will agree that the overlap of personal and firm goals will improve their joint and individual performance. The more that the assigned goals overlap with the personal motivations of the individual being reviewed, the better for everyone.

In simpler terms, if a professional service firm consistently meets its goals over a period of time, it is probably safe to say that a fair proportion of the individuals in the firm are also meeting their personal and business goals. Indeed, it is at the critical and unfortunate point when individual and firm goals begin to seriously diverge that problems arise. When this happens, people as individuals and the firm as a collective entity fail to meet their combined goals. Once this happens, turnover costs, lost business opportunities, and a general decline of the firm will almost certainly follow. However, the key is to maintain a reasonable balance between the individual goals of the separate professionals and the overall goals of the firm. This simply stated objective is the primary function of the performance appraisal process.

Perhaps the key to building an effective performance appraisal form is to keep it simple and flexible. Simplicity in form and function will appeal most to the overachiever behavior type. He sees great value in being uncomplicated and straightforward. The fact that the material is objective and consistent will appeal to his sense of universal fair play, and it will communicate to him that the organization is playing on a level field, where most people are being graded in the same manner. Naturally, even with the same performance appraisal form, some differences will exist. The behavioral differences in managers conducting the performance appraisals can create a difference in ratings, but the overachiever will recognize and accept this. He will also understand and accept the need for *some* flexibility in the rating form.

The presence of flexibility will appeal most to the entrepreneur, active, and aggressive behavior types. The entrepreneur, who is frequently convinced of his own self-importance, thinks that a non-standard document will be semi-created to incorporate his unique talents. This will flatter his ego and may be required in order to accommodate the entrepreneur's ability to react uniquely in different situations. If the entrepreneur shows unique talents that are not generally measured with the existing form, then some accommodation can be made to recognize this situation. The active person sees variety as a meaningful part of life. Sometimes he likes activity and change for its own sake, and he will also endorse the possibility of flexibility in the form. He will not demand or require it, but he will be glad to hear of the possibility.

The aggressive person can, like the entrepreneur, believe that his contribution is unique and should therefore be rated on a separate form. It is not so much the creation of the form that matters to him, as it is the idea that if necessary his contribution can be accommodated with an exception. Conversely, the entrepreneur and aggressive behavior styles prefer the idea of simplicity and simple forms for rating subordinates. This policy allows them to control and influence these people by stating the preferred company policy of using the standard form.

Individuals represented by the passive, sensitized, and compulsive behavior styles are less concerned with the form of the performance appraisal. They assume that it will be designed intelligently and used appropriately. Their approach is in contrast to the entrepreneur and aggressive types because these latter three *do not* see the performance appraisal form as a means to gain more money or status, increased visibility within the firm, or credibility with their superiors. These are goals and incentives for the entrepreneur and aggressive behavior types, who will consciously use any means possible to legitimately advance themselves within the firm.

It is effective to think of the performance appraisal form as having four separate parts: the written evaluation, disagreement addendum, interim summary, and action plan.

Written Evaluation. The written evaluation is a summary evaluation for an individual, covering a specified period of time. It can take many forms. It includes a written evaluation that discusses the performance in some slightly ambiguous verbiage, but also includes a quantitative rating of the person's performance. The quantitative portion is necessary as input for part of the compensation discussion that will follow the performance review. Figure 7.1 depicts one of the most effective means for quantitatively summarizing the performance appraisal review.

The task factors being measured are listed in the far left column. These factors can be changed to suit the position and the company. The factors listed here are obviously sales related, but other equally valid factors can be listed. A second column includes a set of weights that quantify the importance of each factor. These factors are each assigned a weight of between 0 and 1.0, but the total of the weights must equal 1.0. The top portion of the figure is a numerical rating scale ranging from 0 to 1.0. Each candidate is rated on each factor. The final performance rating is determined by multiplying each (weight value) × (the rating scale values) and summing those scores to decide on a performance rating. For example, the task factor "organization" was assigned a task weight of .25. This number is multiplied by the performance rating of .7 for an index of .175. Each of the task factors is assigned a weight and multiplied by the performance rating to give an index figure in a similar fashion. In the example given the total index figure is .450.

Disagreement Addendum. This is a form that allows the person being reviewed to state in writing his disagreement(s) with the review he or she has received. The review will not necessarily be changed, although it can be. At a minimum, the addendum provides the subordinate a chance to express his or her differences with the review received. This addendum can be reviewed by the manager's superior in the firm. If a number of dis-

Figure 7.1
Performance Appraisal Review Rating

TASK FACTORS	WEIGHT	0	.1	.2	.3	.4	.5	.6	.7	.8	.9	1.0	INDEX
Organizing	.25								x				.175
Prospecting	.20					x							.080
Contact	.15			x									.030
Rapport	.15						x						.075
Presentation	.10							x					.060
Follow-up	.10		x										.010
Proposal	.05					x							.020
											TOTAL		.450

agreement addendums are filed against a manager, then it may be an indication that the manager is providing poor leadership to his subordinates. The prime purpose of the disagreement addendum is to provide a check on the performance of the manager.

Interim Summary. This is an official, but less extensive review, of the subordinate. It is completed on an interim basis, preferably the six-month periods between the yearly reviews. The yearly written evaluation review will include areas of needed improvement and suggest ways for the subordinate to improve his or her performance. A six-month period is considered sufficient time for the subordinate to show some positive changes and to warrant an interim review. It should include a reference to the earlier written evaluation review and note where the subordinate's behavior has improved or not changed. Again, it serves as an ongoing basis to evaluate and inform the subordinate of his or her progress.

Action Plan. This is the final part of the structured performance appraisal process. It is a document that is designed to assist the subordinate in achieving goals in a manner that makes sense to him or her. It is intended to be a vehicle that will enable the subordinate to reach his own desired level of performance (with the implied support of the manger). Ideally, the subordinate should write the action plan himself, as an outgrowth of discussions with his manager about what areas need to be improved. He should set his own yardstick of development and measured improvement. This process of buying the subordinate into the review will increase the likelihood that it will be completed successfully.

The exact topics of the performance appraisal should be tailored to the needs of the organization and the level of the person under review. Simplicity and flexibility are important here. The initial review should include performance standards that are reachable and, if possible, jointly decided upon by the subordinate and the manager. This joint decision-making process will increase the likelihood that the goals will be accepted and reached. The interim summary review should take place every six months after the formal performance review. The subordinate needs to know that his manager is still very interested in his development and that the material discussed six months ago is still an important part of the criteria for his review.

The action plan that the subordinate develops should be as specific and task oriented as possible. Definite goals should be established within a given time frame. The purpose of this plan is to show improvement from one review to the next. While these steps sound fairly easy, at least on an intellectual level, their implementation can be difficult.

IMPLEMENTATION

The implementation phase often involves the less mechanical aspects of the plan. It means a face-to-face discussion of the subordinate's behavior and convincing the subordinate to change. If the subordinate cannot or will not accept this advice, then he or she and the manager must face the reality that the firm may not be the best place for that employee. These discussions can be intensely personal, although conducted in the most professional manner, and they often involve a deep understanding of people.

The coaching, counseling, and communication aspects of the performance review process can be difficult. The actual performance feedback session is probably the most difficult part of the whole process for it is intended to modify behavior, assist in professional development, and instill a sense of confidence and motivation in the subordinate. The structural steps to complete this process are well documented in a series of books and manuals on personnel topics. Thus the focus in this text is on the interpersonal aspect of the review process.

The manager who provides performance feedback to different subordinates needs to remember two critical facts: the manager possesses one behavioral style and the subordinate probably possesses a different behavior style. Items that are important to the manager may be less important to the person being reviewed. Therefore, the manager should strive to understand *both* himself and the person he is reviewing. This understanding begins by the manager's categorizing himself or herself in terms of the behavior styles. Before reading further, take the time to graph yourself as a manager—specifically in terms of providing feedback to your subordinates—using Figure 7.2. Next, using the same graph, rate your subordinates.

Figure 7.2
Manager Self-Assessment

SEVEN TRAITS	CATEGORY								
	LOW			MEDIUM			HIGH		
	1	2	3	4	5	6	7	8	9
Overachiever									
Entrepreneur									
Active									
Passive									
Sensitized									
Aggressive									
Compulsive									

Overachiever. The manager who is characterized by the overachiever behavior style can appear unbending, inflexible, moralistic, and intimidating. He may assume that one right way exists to achieve most goals. That path is generally demonstrated by forthright talk and by focusing on tackling problems directly. He is a deliberate and logical person who feels that his brusque fashion is the best way to resolve problems. Such managers are task oriented, focused, no-nonsense, and driven to achieve purposeful goals.

The overachiever manager sees performance review coaching as an opportunity to set the record straight. He sees it as a time that will enable someone to either show his sense of discipline and desire to improve or to resign from the firm. The person whose behavior style is dominated by the overachiever trait can be perceived as too harsh and uncaring. He may be called inflexible and out of touch with today's people.

If these managers have the opportunity to recruit, select, and enlist their "own" people, they have a much higher probability of being successful with them because the overachiever will typically attract and hold people who have a high degree of the same trait. Hence, they will understand each other and develop a sense of rapport with others. However, if the over-achiever manager inherits a group of subordinates with diverse behavioral styles (including moderate to low overachievers), then this condition can cause him and the subordinates some difficulty. They will have problems effectively communicating with each other, and sooner or later one is likely to leave the firm. The manager will probably replace some of the subordinates, rather than leave himself.

The overachiever manager is a disciplined task master, but, in all fairness, he is almost universally perceived to be fair. He does not play favorites, and if his methods are followed, he will almost guarantee success. This type of manager may not necessarily be personally liked by all his subordinates, but he can instill in them a desire to be successful, and he will take the time to demonstrate the "right" way to achieve a series of goals. He is an effective manager from a performance appraisal perspective. He demonstrates a disciplined but consistent, and ultimately successful, manner of developing personnel.

The subordinate who possesses a high degree of the overachiever will warm to this type of supervision like a graduate of U.S. Military Marine Boot-Camp. They may differ on some issues, but they both recognize the value of disciplined training. They may not appear especially chummy, but they will readily show mutual respect. The two overachievers are well matched, and if enough subordinates possess this trait, their manner can build a very disciplined and effective professional unit.

Entrepreneur. The manager who possesses a high degree of the entre-preneur trait will demonstrate a different style of supervision. Generally speaking, for an entrepreneur to reach a managerial role in a professional service firm, he will also demonstrate a reasonably high degree of the overachiever. Such managers are a blend of self-discipline, self-control, and ambition for money and the physical rewards of life. These people are typically interpersonally smooth and socially skilled. They are naturally clever at reading people and possess an almost uncanny ability to read and react to what others are saying in a business or social situation. These people make good managers, but they tend to have a limited degree of patience with the performance review process.

For example, they tend to think that the best people will operate like them—independently and competitively. They are not uncaring, but they do assume that making money is universally recognized as its own reward. They live by the dictum that the more money a person can make (on his own), the better off he will be. They see the invisible hand of competition everywhere and want their subordinates to achieve independence without too much direct supervision from them.

These managers assume that if they are required to "baby-sit" their subordinates, then the subordinates may not be worth keeping. However, their definition of this "sitting" process is considerably shorter compared to other people's definitions. They expect their subordinates to achieve success independently and the overachiever-entrepreneur implies that this is exactly how he achieved his lofty position in the firm. This may be true, but many of these people tend to have a short memory for those who helped them along the way.

The subordinate with a high degree of the entrepreneur trait fits like a hand in glove with the entrepreneur manager. He believes that he has found a manager who is tough on him but who also understands him very well. Because the entrepreneur manager reads people so well, he will readily recognize the less experienced subordinate entrepreneur and take a special, but totally professional interest, in him. They will match and fill each other's needs well. They will typically both prosper together, and the manager will be perceived as a genuine mentor for the subordinate.

Other, more diverse behavior styles will fare reasonably well under the entrepreneur, as long as they show the competitive spirit, self-determination, and semi-Machiavellian insights that the entrepreneur values. Less clever subordinates can feel used and professionally forgotten by such managers. In order to be effective with a wide range of people, this manager needs to understand and accept that not all productive and worthwhile professional people share his sense of immediate reward measured in bonus dollars and business perks.

Active. The manager whose behavior style includes a large portion of the active trait will be everybody's favorite person, at least socially. The person whose behavior style is dominated by the active trait is friendly, personable, and well meaning. He is socially interactive, interested in the give and take of a relationship, and sees value in building long-term relationships. However, the active trait is seldom predominant in an individual behavior style. Frequently, it combines with the passive *or* aggressive traits. It is less frequently combined with the overachiever or entrepreneur traits. The degree to which the active trait combines with each of these other traits will strongly influence the behavior of the manager.

The active-passive behavior style person is at once friendly, personable, and well intentioned, but also slightly unsure, and occasionally tentative. He prefers structure, rules, and some regulations for independence and individual responsibility. He can be a delight to work for because he is easy to work with, generally appreciative of his manager's efforts and results, and is eager to be accepted by the people he is supervising. He is not likely to demand a position of power in the firm, but neither will he be readily courted. In some ways, he is the quintessential middle manager whose career has stalled or is progressing at a very modest rate. He is likeable but cannot score a big success or make a significant impression.

If he could develop slightly more discipline or dynamic energy, then he could reach a position of higher leadership in the firm. He gives insightful, balanced reviews, although generally well within the prescribed limits of raises and promotions. He is not about to rock the boat for anyone, let alone a subordinate. If the recommended salary increase range is from 3 to 5 percent, then his recommendations for raises will be in that range. Everyone likes him personally and professionally, and few people will fault him.

He has the most difficulty supervising individuals with a strong amount of the entrepreneur and aggressive behavior traits. These people will antagonize, fight with, and eventually attempt to undermine his authority. They are anxious for increased visibility in the firm and will not be content remaining in the shadow (as they see their current position) of a person who is not a fighter. In time, such people will either cause the active-passive manager to leave, or will try to transfer away from his work unit and toward a more entrepreneurial or aggressive manager.

Active-Aggressive. The active-aggressive manager stands in sharp contrast to his active-passive counterpart. He, too, is well meaning, likeable, and outwardly friendly. He is also status conscious, occasionally argumentative, and prone to seek out positions of leadership. He welcomes the performance appraisal process. He is not afraid of people and is willing to provide candid, generally inspirational and positive feedback to his subordinates. He sees the responsibility of developing people as a crusade, and he sees himself as being up to the challenge. He does his best to recruit capable individuals and then, like an athletic coach, army drill sergeant, or inspirational teacher, he works with them to improve their present skill level and motivates them to reach goals that, without his unique form of leadership, *might* be beyond their reach.

He is popular with his subordinates because he makes them achieve beyond what they might expect of themselves. He is emotional, persuasive, and friendly—a somewhat charismatic leader—and willing to take the lead on difficult issues. At the same time, he possesses an ego and wants everyone to understand and accept that he is the person in charge. He is the person who dispenses the raises and other corporate perks, and subordinates should recognize that fact. He will be strongly loyal to his subordinates, but he expects the same form of unswerving dedication to whatever course he sets for his unit. He will accept some criticism of his decisions, but he expects everyone to accept his final decisions, and this includes recommendations for raises and promotions.

Subordinates will prosper under his guidance. He may be slightly ostentatious in dress and demeanor. He may also be self-aggrandizing to some degree, but he gets the job done. He will listen to reasonable alternatives, but he will fight for what he believes belongs to his unit. He will share the spoils of his corporate skirmishes with his subordinates but will be inclined to keep a significant portion of the credit for himself. He motivates others effectively and leads by example.

He is not afraid to ask for additional compensation for a subordinate who has proven himself, and he will fight to keep a borderline person who is finally showing signs of improvement. On balance, most people will enjoy working for him, and most will readily recognize that he means well and that they are better off with him than some other manager, at least until they believe that they have outgrown his friendly but ultimately controlling style of supervision.

Passive. The person whose behavior style is dominated by the passive trait may become a manager of a technical unit. Generally, however, he is not likely to play a significant role in developing a unit that is remarkable for its sales or marketing skills. The passive person is compassionate, sympathetic, and interested in doing things in the right way. As a manager of a technical unit, the passive person is cautious, prone to be tentative, and slightly unsure. He lives by the numbers, works according to the rules, and abides by a somewhat strict adherence to company policies and procedures. He does not act this way out of a strong sense of self-discipline, but more from a fear of failure and concern over losing his position.

He will be totally fair, honest, and objective in evaluating his personnel, and they will receive consistent and balanced appraisal for their work. However, they will not necessarily be promoted out of the unit. Their names will not be prominently mentioned, if mentioned at all, as candidates for positions in other departments. He feels somewhat entitled to hold onto the people he thinks he has developed. Besides, he would say, "Why would anyone want to leave here—it's risky making a change, and working for someone else is a big change."

The passive subordinate person will probably be the most submissive in the performance appraisal process. He is not prone to expect too much and, in fact, is predisposed to expect the worst in many situations. An anxiety-inducing process like a work review will probably create a high degree of nervousness and unsteadiness in him. His initial reaction will be complete fear of failure. He will need reassurance and emotional support to overcome these feelings of tentativeness and self-doubt. He needs to be complimented and reassured because with the right form of emotional support and understanding, he can become a dutiful, reliable, and consistently solid performing employee. In marketing-oriented professional service personnel who are involved in a sales activity, the passive trait is most often combined with the active trait to form the active-passive behavior style.

Aggressive. The individual personified by the aggressive behavior style is a commanding, no-nonsense type of person. Again, the aggressive behavior trait seldom demonstrates itself alone. It is most frequently associated with others that form the entrepreneur-aggressive, active-aggressive, or aggressive-compulsive behavior styles.

The aggressive person can be an especially effective leader when combined with any of these behavior traits. The core of the aggressive behavior trait is social dominance, task control, and interpersonal control of most group functions. The key to understanding the aggressive person is to remember that he is driven by emotional insecurity. He needs to control his environment because in that way it cannot attack him. He wants to be in charge so that his authority will not be usurped by some outside source.

He strives to be fair and evenhanded in providing performance feedback, but he also aspires to ensure a sense of loyalty tinged with dependence from his subordinates. He strives to influence his subordinates so that their primary loyalty is to him first and to the firm as an organization second. In that way, if he should "need" them for anything, they will see him in a positive light. The one area where he may need them is if he decides to leave the firm; in this case, he may try to persuade some of his former subordinates to leave with him. In his mind, the subordinates will work with him in a subordinate role in a new firm (possibly his own). The organization needs to safeguard against this possibility.

The aggressive subordinate can be a socially combative subordinate in the performance review process. It is wise to prepare thoroughly for the session with him and to marshal the facts with irrevocable substantiation for the comments made. He is prone to debate any negative comments and can take such remarks in a personal manner far more than might be expected.

Sensitized. The person characterized by the sensitized behavior style who also happens to be a manager in a marketing-oriented firm is unusual. He may hold a high-level technical (R & D) or specialized administrative function, but seldom a marketing-oriented managerial post. However, the sensitized manager is uniquely well qualified to read, evaluate, and understand the behavior nuances of his subordinates. He is highly perceptive about people and uncannily deductive in terms of understanding the motivations behind seemingly contradictory behavior.

However, as credible and capable as the sensitized person is in reading people, he typically lacks the social charisma or leadership qualities to utilize these skills to purposefully direct and lead people—except in a technical area. He is creative, original, insightful, and genuinely thoughtful but lacks the outward sense of self-confidence to take charge of situations and become a dynamic leader. He almost instinctively knows what should be done and can support and assist another person's lead, but he frequently lacks the outward sense of socialization to be an effective leader himself.

As a subordinate, the sensitized person will quietly accept his performance review rating and surmise that he has or has not been treated fairly. If he decides that he is not being given a reasonable reward for his efforts, he seldom will voice his complaints but will surely seek employment elsewhere, and once focused on another position, he will not be deterred from leaving the firm. Managers can make the mistake of assuming that because the sensitized person is quiet and self-effacing, that he lacks belief in himself. Actually, the sensitized person frequently thinks of himself as superior but feels no need to outwardly broadcast his inner self-assurance. However, he also feels that if his manager is not sufficiently perceptive to recognize his talents, then he will quietly plan to leave his present situation for a new one.

Compulsive. The person categorized by the compulsive behavior style is statistically rare in society. Yet when observed, his behavior pattern is quite obvious. In some ways, the mechanical, logical, and quietly well-meaning Mr. Spock of *Star Trek* is the prototype of this person. He is equally interested in the fairness and logic of the appraisal process as he is in the final rating he receives. As he perceives the process, if the material used to prepare the appraisal is rational, then the conclusions will ultimately be fair. He may argue about the logic of a certain conclusion, but he will seldom show much emotion about the final analysis. Eventually, if he agrees with most of the points, he will decide that it was a fair process. If not, he will conclude that such subjective processes as performance appraisals are inherently subjective and that he just has to learn to live with the results.

COMPENSATION

Compensation in all its forms—pay, benefits, perks, stock options, and so on—is an integral part of the professional person's employment package. Moreover, compensation plays a vital role in developing and motivating the members of the firm. It may not be popular to highlight the single importance of compensation and rewards in a professional service firm, but the bottom line is that compensation plays an integral role in building a professional service organization.

Many studies have been conducted to show the "reduced" importance of compensation. For business people, in general two frequently cited theories are Abraham Maslow's impressive theory on the hierarchy of needs and Frederick Herzberg's two-factor theory of motivation. Both these popular theories report impressive results, and like many academic studies, they also have opponents who cast aspersions on their validity. Nonetheless, they are well known and are frequently quoted in the popular business press. The authors of both of these studies and the hundreds of other studies that are based on their results, or are similar to them in using scientific methods, did not analyze the behavior styles of the people they studied. The studies included large groups of professional, administrative, research, and even blue-collar workers but did not separate the participants according to behavior style. The work reported here suggests that when the behavior styles of the individuals involved in the studies are analyzed, different results emerge. That is, while to certain behavior styles compensation is especially important, to other behavior styles, it is much less important.[1] This is to be expected.

However, the behavior styles that are the most likely to be successful in a marketing-oriented professional service organization are frequently highly motivated by compensation. These behavior styles include individuals who are high on the overachiever, entrepreneurial, and aggressive traits. People who score high on the overachiever trait see compensation in two ways, first, as a way of keeping score, and second, as a way of partially measuring their worth in the marketplace. The entrepreneur is interested in compensation because he is primarily money motivated. He sees value in having a higher income and is willing to work hard in order to achieve it. The aggressive person is interested in compensation as a means of securing the status and prestige that he aspires to, but also as a way of securing his place in the hierarchy of the firm.

When focusing on the more marketing-oriented people who are successful in a professional service firm, money talks. This is not to deny the importance of other issues that are critical to successful marketing-oriented professional people, but compensation is a consistently important factor to the better people. This issue should be recognized and dealt with, not swept aside as some potentially embarrassing side issue. Again, not all the successful personnel are only money driven, but it does play a significant role.

Compensation is also an important factor to individuals whose behavior styles emphasize other traits. The individuals whose behavior is typified by the active, passive, sensitized, and compulsive behavior styles are typically less interested in compensation per se than their counterparts. Money is important to them, but it is typically no more important than a host of other factors. However, in studying the professional service firm, it is important to understand the people characterized by these traits and their level of interest in compensation as well.

Compensation and the professional employee is a broad-based and encompassing topic. Many books have been written on the technical aspects of it. The focus here is more restrictive. Compensation is evaluated below in terms of three different criteria—recruitment, reward, retention—and the seven behavior styles in the professional service firm.

Recruitment. Financial reward is a significant factor for most people who enter the field of professional services. This is especially true for people joining the ranks of a professional service firm for the first time or those changing firms within an industry. The truth of this is easily seen in the fact that large professional firms (including law firms and consulting firms), routinely start "new" professional personnel at the same high salary. This is not done out of the goodness of their hearts but because they want to limit their initial expenditure for somewhat unproven talent and do not want to begin a bidding war with each other for the same pool of talent.

The people who choose professional services as a career frequently are intelligent, well educated (MBAs, lawyers, actuaries, etc.), and disciplined. They have proven themselves over a period of years, although in the somewhat rarified atmosphere of school and limited professional employment. They believe in their own worth, and this self-perception has been reinforced by the flattering recruiting treatment they receive from the firms seeking to employ them. They have some definite expectations concerning their work load and their rewards for a career in the field. They also make conscious choices (at least they would like to think they are deliberate) about the type of firms for which they choose to work.

Once employed, they also anticipate continuing their self-imposed regimen. They expect to work long, hard hours and to be compensated for working under pressure and with strict production deadlines. They would like to think that their sense of social maturity and business judgment is important—and it *is* to some degree—but these traits will be developed over time as they gain an opportunity to ascend in the firm's hierarchy and as they take on increased responsibilities for marketing the firm's products and services.

The dollar amount for a starting position is important to most professional service personnel, but since this is largely determined and partially controlled by the market forces of supply and demand, it is relatively set. However, the type of compensation will quickly separate the incoming professional service personnel: salary; salary and bonus; or salary, bonus, and commission.

The more passive individuals will strongly prefer the straight salary for compensation, whereas the more entrepreneurial and aggressive personnel will be more inclined to seek some form of salary and bonus or commission. They believe in "controlling" their destiny to a greater degree and are more willing to invest in themselves as a means of achieving their goals. Interestingly, the active person is probably the most flexible, and he can be sold on the idea of a bonus/commission compensation package easier than the other behavior styles.

Reward. In the best of all possible worlds, the most productive workers receive the biggest rewards. However, employees frequently feel that, despite their own self-rated importance and sense of work dedication, this is not the case. For those employed in a marketing-oriented professional service firm, there is a greater likelihood of being able to reach that level of mental equilibrium. Like sales personnel anywhere, the more business the professional person performs, the more credit he can claim. Hence, he can, with some degree of assurance, correlate his individual productivity, defined as billable hours or new business, with his compensation. This direct link between productive work and compensation is not lost on anybody.

The key issue becomes the definition of productive work. Should productive work be measured in effort extended or by specifiable task accomplishments? Such tasks are typically actual billable hours, or new clients who start using the firm due to a single person's efforts. In the case of the latter criteria, are rewards issued on the basis of presentations made or by the number of new clients who actually begin using the firm's products and services? On the one hand, some people could argue that it is important and even necessary to give a number of presentations before expecting any new clients, and therefore the number of presentations alone is the key variable. This argument is most frequently put forward by people with the active or active-passive behavior style. These people are prone to see that their efforts are worth rewarding and perceive that the long-term goals of the firm are best served by keeping as many people happy as possible. They see long term goals in terms of building relationships with clients over time. Whoever happens to present when a client "buys," is less important than the fact that several people presented to the clients. They would argue that it is very difficult and sometimes impossible to determine which presentation or presenter was most influential, that clients are impressed with the firm as a whole (based on their perception of all the professional people), and that individual credit for a particular presentation is less valid than a total team achievement. Thus, they are inclined to reward "effort" almost as much as results.

Other equally experienced management personnel will justly argue that the number of presentations by itself is of limited value. It is the number of clients who actually begin to use the firm following a presentation that should be used as the only valid criterion for productive work. These people suggest that a person who makes a large number of presentations per sale is actually losing a large number of potential clients and clearly is doing something wrong. Effort per se, they argue, and especially this type of effort, should not be rewarded. Only those professional people who deliver tangible, revenue-generating presentations should receive financial rewards. This scenario defines prospective client presentations as a scarce resource and demonstrates that the firm is hurt by poor presentations.

This argument is presented by people with an entrepreneur, aggressive, or entrepreneur-aggressive behavior style. These people are competitive, driven, and focused on the rights and responsibilities of the individual as a sole contributor. They would use professional sports teams (baseball, football, basketball, hockey, etc.) for an analogy. These people would argue that every player on the team earns a solid salary because every player on the team contributes to the overall accomplishment of the team. However, they would also point out that each player is measured by his individual contribution to the team effort.

Moreover, they would suggest that the "better" players earn more money because they make greater individual contributions, and they should be rewarded for those contributions. In order to carry the analogy back to the world of professional services, they would argue that the person who actually signs up an existing or new client for a new project deserves a larger share of any bonus credit for his efforts. These people work on the principle that the results are the most meaningful measure of contribution, and that individual results can be measured in any team activity, including marketing professional services.

These scenarios are not meant to be taken as the only possible means of allocating credit for a sales presentation. However, they are fairly typical of the types of group versus individual rewards that arise in professional services organizations. Both sides of the issue have merit, and both sides raise concerns. The first group-oriented rewards process assumes that everyone is equally skilled, motivated, and disciplined to deliver the best possible presentation. Clearly, this is seldom true.

Conversely, the reward system that reinforces individual efforts can result in a situation where everyone works primarily for their own welfare and seldom thinks of the greater benefit of the group. People can become so focused on gathering their self-described bonus points, that they refuse to cooperate with others on even the simplest of tasks. Moreover, once a client does sign a contract, they are more focused on cornering some share of the sales credit than in producing the work to complete the project. So both of these extremes have some inherent problems. A possible solution is to build in joint rewards and to reward individual efforts.

Retention. The relationship of compensation to retention is almost a straight correlation between behavior style and retention. To the over-achiever, the compensation package, however divided between dollars, perks, and benefits, is a direct reflection of the firm's perception of his contribution. He does not work directly for money and in some ways would be offended if someone suggested that this was his motivation. He works for the pleasure of accomplishing his goals. Nevertheless, he expects to be rewarded for his achievements. He will be understanding if he contributes a solid performance for several years and is not directly rewarded for his specific contribution. He will accept the explanation that the firm as a whole had a bad year and that everyone is expected to pull together and build for the future. He will accept and abide by this rule for some time. However, if he sees what he considers to be unwise investments or perks being distributed to others—when he made a definable contribution and was not rewarded—he will leave the firm on principle. Once he announces his resignation, no amount of increased money, prestige, or perks is likely to renew his interest in the organization.

The entrepreneur follows the theory that "behavior, like water, seeks its own level"—meaning of course, that the more pressure that is applied to the water or behavior, the higher it will rise. He deliberately places pressure on himself to achieve definable goals. Correspondingly, he expects to be rewarded for having done so. He does not ask for rewards for his efforts, but he can demand payment for his results. He is a money-motivated person and is likely to leave the ship quickly at the first sign of trouble. He is loyal to himself, and he sees no reason to stay with a potentially sinking ship. The only event that assures his retention is the constant flow of compensation.

The active person is an emotionally loyal person. He will remain part of the team for as long as he has personal ties with the firm. He is not especially motivated to stay or leave by compensation alone. For him, it is a matter of making new friends in a new firm that will prove troublesome. "Why should I leave my friends for a few more dollars," he would jovially ask? "To me," he would respond, "the firm is like a home, and I see no reason to leave for a small increment in pay."

The passive person is frequently the last person to leave. An increase in compensation would, to him, entail an increase in responsibility. Generally speaking, this is not a positive inducement. He makes "enough" with the present firm and is not inclined to leave for more money. If the firm is doing poorly, he may be inclined to leave for more security, but money per se is not a prime motivator with him. Also, he is not likely to leave of his own accord even if he is performing poorly. He may have to be terminated. He is afraid of change, and has a difficult time deciding on issues. Action on his part has to be forced.

The aggressive person can be surprising on this issue. If he is also high on the entrepreneur trait, then he will be cleverly calculating his financially optimal time to leave. If he is high on the overachiever or active trait, he can prove stubbornly loyal to the firm. Money will become a secondary issue in retaining him. The opportunity for advancement and an increase in organizational power, perks, and visibility are almost more important to him. He aspires to the corner office—with its attendant status—and only secondarily to the accumulation of wealth and financial security.

The sensitized person is typically thought to be the least interested in compensation of all the behavior types. On the surface this is true. However, the sensitized person is interested in some idealized notion of fairness with regard to compensation and many other issues. If he feels that he is being deliberately underpaid compared to others in the firm, then he will be sorely tempted to leave. So he is not so much greedy or anxious about making more money for himself, as he is sensitive about being treated as an inferior team member. Almost more than financial compensation, some selected perks, like state-of-the-art equipment, opportunities to attend professional conventions, and an atmosphere that rewards the pursuit of creative ideas, are important to the sensitized person. So although compensation in general, and money in particular, are not of singular importance to him, the sensitized person is affected by the distribution of compensation perks. He wants his self-perceived fair share or he will leave.

The compulsive person projects the same general feelings about compensation as the overachiever. He is concerned with the perceived fairness and validity of the distribution. He is not motivated by money or other benefits alone, and an increase of X percent will not motive him to stay or leave. However, it is the overall sense of logic and rationality behind the rewards that will tie him to an organization.

NOTE

1. These findings were reported in James B. Weitzul, *Sales Force Dynamics: Motives, Management, Money, Marketplace* (Westport, Conn.: Quorum Books, 1993).

Chapter Eight

LEADERSHIP: MANAGERS AND MANAGEMENT

Today, if a professional person performs positively in his present position, he is rewarded for that performance with consistent raises in compensation and increases in responsibility within his particular job function. In time, he can be promoted to a higher position and begin the cycle all over again. Eventually, he will reach a position of management. This was previously not always the case. A generation ago, the professional service firm executives appointed a top or senior consultant as the manager, without much thought, but this notion that the best consultant makes the best manager is gone. His success with clients, managing technical projects, or selling the technical expertise of others does not necessarily endow him with the wisdom of a manager.

Professional service firm marketing management today is both a profession and an art. It requires more ability and skill than in previous eras. Professional service firm managers face complex responsibilities with diverse products and intricate marketing techniques. They interpret computer data, as well as expense tabs. With many mergers and rapid corporate expansions, the transition from the consultant post to the manager's chair requires sophisticated adaptation.

When thrust into management, some people reach the limits of their capabilities: some remain stuck in their attitude and habit patterns. Some may enjoy consulting because of personal contacts but fail to keep up with the report writing and need for change when shifting to the role of manager. A consultant may have difficulty in the transition from the forward line to sitting on the coach's bench. The ability to shift in attitude determines the success of those aspiring to professional service firm management. This transition is almost always difficult for anyone moving into management for the first time, and it is especially hard for a successful consultant.

MANAGERS

If we examine an effective consultant, we might wonder why he wanted to become a manager. He enjoys many facets of consulting: the power of persuasion, each customer conquest, direct interaction, personal contact, and direct control of a given client base or technical area. Why would he want to change? The effective consultant, however, looks for new challenges to test his competitive drive. It is challenging to swap the tangibility of product development or marketing for intangible personnel decisions and responsibility for the development of others. He sheds the familiar past for an uncertain future.

Some who accept this challenge expect that management will involve little change. Yet the successful consultant actively courts change. For the consultant who has become a manager, shifts in attitudes and habits will be the greatest challenge. While action and behavior require change, attitude and value predetermine action and make any subsequent change lasting. Detecting the person with ready potential for change and developing that potential is not easy. But that is what making managers out of consultants is all about.

Why bother with a difficult transition? Why not hire a seasoned manager from outside? This alternative is practical when there is no available successor who could rapidly grow into the job. If such hiring substitutes for staff development, it can be disastrous in the long run, however. Successful professional firms would be undermined. First, professional personnel would lose morale. Second, there are few effectively seasoned middle managers. Third, companies reduce problems by training managers to fit their unique situations.

Building future managers from within a firm allows the manager to enjoy helping people advance. Managers may enjoy prestige, money, and power, but if they do not pride themselves in building subordinates, they have not made the transition. They will miss much of the fun of management. The manager selects from those who say they are interested in management, but all may not really mean it. All recruits will probably say that they want responsibility, challenge, and a chance to develop people. But their motivations will differ and their performance will show this. A manager also should not overlook the consultant who says, "No, I'd rather not be a manager, thank you." While this person may be realistic in his ambitions and self-assessment, he might underrate himself. It might be that he could blossom quickly with the right exposure and direction. With this exception, a manager usually chooses from those actively seeking the position.

This decision depends on the manager's intuition about the candidate's readiness to switch attitudes and learn. The steady, rock-like career of the technically oriented professional person and unofficial part-time supervisor is worth his weight in gold, but he may be too set in his ways to cope with the complexities of the management process. The cocky, independent, and impulsive consultant may be a good long-term prospect, but he may not yet be ready. He would need coaching to help him mature. The first candidate is successful but static; the second, immature but changing.

What signs separate the self-centered consultant from one who has a feeling for fellow consultants? How can one gauge a readiness to shift attitudes from personal accomplishment to responsibility for others? What identifies the desirable supervisor and manager? No single characteristic in the prospective consultants will solve the manager's selection problem. Professional service managers will need different guidelines for selecting potential managers, depending on their own temperament, the products they market, and the companies they represent. Evidence from these and other sources must be gathered before making decisions. Despite these different needs, some areas demonstrate common aspects worth noting.

The most basic characteristic that any potentially successful marketing-oriented professional service manager must have is a solid level of the overachiever trait. If the manager possesses sufficient discipline, control, task motivation, and self-sufficiency—as defined by the overachiever trait—then he will be successful. The overachiever manager demonstrates a desire to grow. Rather than just talking about self-improvement, he seeks performance appraisals and criticism from superiors. He takes suggestions seriously that might aid consultant effectiveness or management responsibility. He volunteers for courses that provide new skills and reads broadly to gain new perspectives. He learns how to evaluate his own efforts and finds self-correcting devices to promote personal growth.

While thinking cannot solve all management problems, it can help. The quality of managerial thinking can be estimated by the thinking style of the person in question. Does he solve problems emotionally or analytically? Is he conventional or original? Does he think strictly for himself or in the best interest of the group? Does he become broader in thinking, or more narrow?

Ideally, the manager possesses a high degree of the overachiever trait and a high degree of intelligence. Such a person is both emotionally disciplined and intellectually quick. He can readily see the implications of his plans and actions, and he possesses the ability to validly interpret the plans of others. However, sufficiently high levels of the overachiever trait can compensate for a person's lacking significant levels of other characteristics, including a high level of intelligence. This is not to deny the importance of raw reasoning ability in the marketing-oriented manager. However, it is important to recognize that with sufficient self-discipline, even a person of average or higher reasoning ability can be an effective professional service marketing-oriented manager. This is primarily true because the person also possesses the self-confidence to recruit and select people who possess more natural intelligence than he has. Although more intelligent, these people also possess less focused drive to accomplish the firm's goals than the reasonably intelligent (but not necessarily brilliant) overachiever.

Overachiever. As a manager, the overachiever brings his sense of focus, discipline, and dedication to achievement to the group. He sets high goals and expects the team to achieve them—with himself setting a prime example of the work ethic he expects. He leads by doing. He may not necessarily have a full and detailed knowledge of all the technical or even the administrative or sales requirements of the group he is leading. Others may know more than he does about a particular operation of the unit; however, his example of self-discipline, direct communication, and no-nonsense approach will serve as an overall model for professionals with varied degrees of expertise.

Generally, he will have one specialty area, such as administrative, sales, or technical. He will use his superior knowledge or ability in this one area as a source of credibility for his overall leadership in all areas. He will be knowledgeable of the other areas but will rely on experts in those areas for primary input.

His interpersonal management style is somewhat brusque, until he is familiar with his peers and subordinates. Even then, his sense of internal discipline will prevent him from becoming too familiar with people. He will, however, develop a reputation for treating everyone fairly. He likes to think of himself as the ultimate judge of "rational" behavior.

He may start out a little slower than some others in the sales area. This is because although he is thoroughly disciplined and motivated to achieve his goals, he can come across as somewhat cold and intimidating. He may be accused of not knowing the meaning of the word *compromise* and insisting (perhaps too consistently) that projects be completed *his* way. However, once clients feel comfortable with his ramrod-straight approach to problem solving, they will accept his overall demeanor and somewhat formal presentation style. In dealing with clients, he is seen as a level-headed, thorough, and methodical professional who constantly seeks to place the welfare of the client ahead of his own personal or corporate agenda. For this reason, his judgment is generally implicitly trusted and his recommendations are readily endorsed.

Entrepreneur. Those professionals likely to advance in the firm are profit oriented. The behavior trait most associated with direct ambition for increased profits is the entrepreneur. However, if the entrepreneur's orientation is selfish, and if he lacks sufficient levels of the overachiever trait, the person will remain a lone consultant and not become a manager. If the entrepreneur includes all those involved in the venture, he may be considered for management. If he is personally interested in covering territory, profits, advertising effectiveness, and other factors influencing the return on the dollar, then he probably possesses a solid degree of the entrepreneurial trait. Another indication of the entrepreneur is his ability to read people, especially in the recruiting process.

Every manager does some recruiting. The entrepreneurial manager is selective and perceptive in referring professional candidates. He demonstrates insight into people and the causes of behavior. He is selective. He has learned to identify qualities that dispose others to success in the firm, especially in the sales and marketing functions. Typically, the managerial strength of the entrepreneur is in the sales and marketing area. He is less interested in administrative functions because he believes that he can cost-effectively delegate these activities to a subordinate. Remember, monetary achievement is his prime motivation and so he tends to think of activities in terms of cost-benefit ratios.

If the entrepreneurial manager is also highly intelligent, he may have an interest in some practical, useful, and marketable products for the firm, and he may have developed some of them. He will have completed the research for these products with an eye toward marketing them throughout the firm, and they may well be highly successful. However, it is more likely that he worked on a team that developed the products, and he is now claiming a significant portion of the credit for the overall product.

His management and interpersonal styles tend to be somewhat short-term in nature. His focus is immediate payback, and he is typically less interested in developing long-term relationships. He partially sees people as instruments to accomplish his personal ends, and he manages his interpersonal and client relationships to that end. Some subordinates may accurately interpret his minimalist management style as appropriate for them because they share his individualistic orientation, while others will prefer a more proactive approach to their supervision.

In a similar vein, some clients will approve of his competitive nature, his willingness to negotiate prices for services, and his entrepreneurial interpersonal style. They will relish working with him personally because he delivers his product under fear of being out-sold by a competitor. Other clients will prefer a more traditional service approach. Some people will take to him like a duck to water, primarily because they admire his apparent sense of business acumen, street smarts, and competitive drive. Others will find him distasteful and cite these very same characteristics. If a manager is merely seen as a competitor, then he is not likely to make a good manager. He needs to combine the competitive drive of the entrepreneur with the discipline of the overachiever to be a truly productive professional service manager.

Active. In direct contrast to the previous type of managerial behavior, the active behavior style is helpful to fellow workers in complimenting those who do well, volunteering tips, and sharing mistakes. At meetings, the active person reaches out to new professionals, offering warmth, understanding, and assistance through the introductory and probationary periods. He helps the new person feel wanted as part of the group. The candidate also expresses appreciation to the staff, for instance, in smoothing a customer complaint. Moreover, he shares the credit with his peers when excelling in client development activities.

The active manager demonstrates a high degree of flexibility, intellectual curiosity, team courage, and group judgment. All these attributes and more are needed to cope with difficult management decisions. The active manager is cooperative, welcomes new products, has courage, and lives with change.

These traits may make him seem like a capable administrator. If the overachiever trait is high, then he can be a solid administrator; however, this is generally not the case. In a similar way, if his intelligence level is high, he may be adept at product development. But his most frequent contribution to the firm is in the area of people and sales management. He is something of a natural at interacting with others. He generally forms a positive impression of others. Everyone knows him and most people genuinely like him. He manages others the way he would like to be supervised. He is open, considerate, and well meaning. He is focused on the team and interested in achieving goals that will benefit everyone. He may claim a large portion of the reward when a task is accomplished, but typically he will also be among the first to forgo his due in difficult times. He lives for the team and is inspired by and dedicated to achieving group goals.

Clients duly appreciate the active manager. They see him as a person who consistently provides good service with a positive attitude. He is

"Johnny on the spot," with accurate information and a pleasant demeanor. He likes people contact and thrives on client relationship building. Clients are pleased to work with him and are sometimes eager to refer him to other prospective clients. Most clients instinctively know when they are asking for extra attention, but the active manager obligingly provides it. He may need to be reminded to invoice the client for extra services, but once called, he delights in being able to help a friend who happens to be a fee-paying client.

Passive. The manager with a dominant passive behavioral style is rare. The passive trait may be present in the person's overall behavior style, but it is very unusual for the predominantly passive person to reach a managerial position. When it does occur, it usually happens because the person possesses some significant technical expertise and expertise in nominally supervising a technical group of people. More likely, the person will have been in a support role for a long period of time, generally for a very successful person who suddenly leaves the managerial position, and the passive person is mistakenly promoted because of his assumed capabilities.

The inherent passivity, cautiousness, and tentativeness of the passive person will severely limit his capacity for success in a managerial role. Further, pressure for increased results, production, sales, or even a tight time frame for delivering a report, can bring out some form of negative behavior in the passive manager. This can take the form of an emotionally negative outburst that will dampen the most enthusiastic of subordinate personnel. Even those managers whose behavior style is partially passive can have a difficult time in the managerial role. The most frequent behavior type of this sort is the active-passive, and this style will be discussed later.

Sensitized. The most self-aware person is represented by the behavior style of the sensitized manager. The stability of a budding manager in directing others depends upon his inner strength, personal security, and ability to project that strength and security to others. He may be judged by how he thinks, communicates, desires to grow, and projects his self-image. At first glance, the sensitized person does not appear to be especially strong or independent. This is generally true for the sensitized trait by itself. However, when combined with a high degree of the overachiever and a high degree of intelligence, the sensitized person may be very capable of becoming a successful manager.

The overachiever sensitized manager disciplines himself in the little details. In the marketing/sales process, he controls himself in order to handle difficult prospects and does not become a mere order taker. He knows his products and services well and is knowledgeable and frequently highly creative about how to apply them to different client situations. He is also a capable office administrator. His sense of urgency helps him manage time effectively. He can appear to be dreaming or considering some abstract application of his ideas, but in reality he will be anticipating and planning for everyday office situations. He is highly perceptive in dealing with people and often understands their critical issues before they can verbalize them. Moreover, he may appear stoic, diffident, and even aloof from his subordinates in an administrative role, but he does care about them. This sense of concern will manifest itself in ways that are not immediately apparent to the staff.

His interpersonal management style is largely one of freedom. He is not an aggressive, controlling person and prefers to manage the way he likes to be supervised—with a great deal of personal freedom but also a reasonable safety net for emergencies. Often, his technical skills are superb. He is, by definition, creative, original, and insightful about technical matters and can readily see the critical issues that are the foundation of a large-scale project. He may have difficulty gathering sufficient emotional energy to persuasively present his insights. However, he frequently is crystal clear in his thinking and once allowed or encouraged to speak his mind, the laser sharp brightness of his ideas can readily penetrate the densest fog surrounding an idea. For this reason alone, clients will come to enjoy his presentations and will anticipate seeing him unravel a complex problem into a set of routine issues. He develops relationships based on technical merit, not social friendliness, and he develops patterns of friendship over time. However, his clients and subordinates will be intensely loyal to him, primarily because he is eager to promote the value of the best idea, regardless of the person presenting it.

While marketing professional services depends upon individual effort, managing has no meaning apart from people. Potential managers should evaluate their attitudes toward others, especially new associates, technical staff, superiors, and other workers. The sensitized manager is uncommon in a marketing-oriented professional service organization. However, he is frequently also intelligent and disciplined. These secondary factors enable him to politely push his ideas and repeatedly gain an appreciative audience for his technical wizardry and calming client interaction skills.

Aggressive. This person will act like someone of stature, and he is ready to take his place in the upper echelons of management whenever called upon. He keeps top management informed of his progress. He welcomes his immediate superior's comments on his performance. He takes directions and asks for clarification when directions are vague. He uses his manager's guidance and absorbs others' good habits in order to be a useful consultant and future manager.

He is frequently an adept administrative manager. He sees administration of his group as a means of control, and he is inspired to control whatever group he can. He may not be especially liked by his subordinates because he is such a strong controlling influence, but he is a capable administrative manager, and he will be respected by most everyone. Typically, marketing and sales are his strength. He readily sees increased market share as the means to increase the speed of his own climb up the corporate ladder. Although he may be especially sensitive to rejection, and frustrated when clients do not accept his advice, he can be a diligent sales person and will not easily be dissuaded from achieving his goals, sales or otherwise.

The aggressive's interpersonal style can be intimidating and deliberate. He is suspicious of the motives of other people, and he tends to act first and ask questions later. If sufficiently controlled, he can be a dynamic sales person. He does not readily take "no" for an answer, and he is inspiring because he believes in his cause and will preach about it with charisma and vigor. He is determined to win and wants to be considered the source of worthwhile information. He is jealous of his client relationships and will cover his clients with services to ensure his entry in to their upper echelons. His style of management is dynamic and controlling. Clients will feel "safe" in his presence for he will have carefully researched the alternatives, and his recommendations will be based on sound reasoning and will be persuasively presented. He is a capable manager because he inspires loyalty in his subordinates and delivers projects for them to complete. At the same time, he is motivated to climb the ladder ever higher and will readily develop those people who are loyal to him.

Compulsive. Few sales/marketing-oriented professional service personnel show zeal for routine *and* the details of selling. The person typified by the compulsive trait, however, does. The compulsive trait is seldom seen by itself; it is most often combined with other traits. Most commonly it combines with the aggressive trait. When this happens, the manager is both charismatic and systematic. He can effectively woo an audience with a sales presentation and come back to the office and immediately produce a lengthy proposal for the client.

The compulsive trait is also worthwhile in itself. Most managers procrastinate with correspondence, record keeping, report writing, and other chores apart from direct personal contact. The compulsive manager, however, has mastered managerial routine. He knows what has to be done after a customer places an order. He checks the progress of the order and provides service after the product arrives. He also knows that the welfare of fellow consultants, management, and the customer depend upon this execution of managerial routines.

He also demonstrates skill in direct, uncomplicated, and literal communication, especially in client relationships. He conveys thoughts clearly to customers, peers, and superiors. He rarely uses sarcasm and never undercuts a fellow professional. He does not offer the "last word" of criticism, nor does he helpfully interpret and interrupt others by finishing their sentences. He operates in a direct and no-nonsense manner. He is an administrative creature and sees value in order and systems. His clients enjoy his sense of systematic thinking and logical deduction. However, they may require some time to "warm up" to him interpersonally. It is almost as if he spends so much time functioning in a methodical fashion that he has little emotional energy left for the more traditional forms of social interaction.

This list of trait discussions may seem long, but selecting a manager should include all these and more. Obvious possible combinations of trait patterns have not been presented here as potential managers. However, these combinations have been presented in other parts of the book. Moreover, the talent hunt should involve looking for patterns and change in consultants. Value shifts and attitudinal changes should be noted. Does the potential manager move toward people and involvement with them? Does he need external support for stimulation and a highly structured set of instructions? Is he a capable leader of professionals?

MANAGEMENT

The previous section focused on the behavior traits and responsibilities associated with being a successful manager. This section will develop those thoughts into actions and review some of the behaviors that managers engage in to improve the performance of their people. Most managers in professional service organizations readily acknowledge the importance of effective management. At the same time, there is limited agreement on the exact definition of effective management. In a general sense, everyone accepts that it means accomplishing goals through people and necessarily includes the traditional rubrics of planning, coordinating, directing, and reviewing the activities of subordinates.

In the context of managing professional subordinates, these standard textbook themes are useful but also somewhat bland and general. "After all," some professional managers proclaim, "we are managing fellow professionals, not supervising people on an assembly line. The traditional

Management 101 rules do not readily apply to us or our situation." Perhaps. In some sense it can be argued that this is a valid criticism and that the more standard approaches simply do not work as effectively with professional people, and especially in a marketing-oriented environment. In the emotionally charged, achievement pressurized, and highly independent atmosphere that exists in a marketing-oriented professional service organization, *leadership* may be a more appropriate one-word description than management. This simple change in terminology also entails a rethinking of philosophy. Leadership requires that the manager influence his professional staff in roughly the same way that professional personnel influence their clients. Using this approach, the professional manager is required to politely direct the professional person toward a series of goals that are compatible with the person and the firm. This is a more ethereal task and subject to pitfalls. One of the key pitfalls is a matter of perception. The professional person *can* be perceived in this situation as a passive object being manipulated by a clever manager into performing a series of acts. In some ways, this perception is similar to the idea that the consultant can unceremoniously lead his clients to act in a way that is contradictory to their own best interests. This assumption simply does not hold water. Almost by definition, no professional person can be misled into performing unprofessionally. True, people can be influenced, but this is different from being manipulated. People are influenced, consciously or not, everyday.

Different environmental and social factors will cause people to react to situations differently. This is a function of being an adult in the business world. It is not manipulation. If people are influenced to act in a way that is not in their best interest, then they will come to see their mistakes and change their behavior or their environment. A brief encounter with negative influences is possible, but it is also generally impossible to maintain over a long period of time, and most professional relationships are based on long-term mutual advantage. In a fairly short period of time, the mutual advantages of operating in a certain manner should be obvious to both the manager and the professional person.

In the final analysis, the effective management of professional people is an individual enterprise. Certain general rules of management apply, but the effective management of marketing-oriented professional people is a one-on-one activity. This is not because the people are prima donnas; they are not. They do, however, possess unique talents that are worth recognizing. The developing person and the established better ones typically have a host of options to consider. They are on the verge of becoming "free agents."

In simple terms, people are treated as individuals because they possess unique skills and abilities. They do not operate in a closed system. The opening in the business environment is called alternative employment. If they are not pleased with their treatment in one atmosphere, they can easily change their business environment for a different employer. After all, prize professional athletes are not treated simply as tools; they are treated like the valuable money-making people they are. Why should professional people be any different?

Ideally, the professional person's initiative, drive, motivation and other positive characteristics should be intrinsic to him. However, it is the responsibility of the manager to select people with these traits and then add to whatever level the person possesses to reach an even greater realization of his potential. The manager can only improve the existing resources of the person. He cannot give him the minimal level of characteristics required to qualify for the race. The manager cannot instill in the professional person what he lacks in basic skills. However, the best managers can recognize the inherent abilities of the individual and build on them in such a way that the person, the manager, and the firm all gain a respectable return on investment.

It has been found that even in what is defined as a very positive work environment, many people will still only perform up to the minimal required workload. These people perform at the level they believe is required to keep their position. Strangely, in some circumstances even money is not a sufficient motivator to increase production. However, this mood can dramatically change once new management techniques are introduced. Time and time again, it has been shown that the manager is the most important influence on a marketing-oriented work force.

The best environment in which to manage marketing-oriented professionals is the field, seeing real prospective clients and delivering a proposal or presentation. However, numerous intermediate steps (and opportunities for failure) exist between this "final" presentation and the first opportunity to meet a prospective client. The manager should be aware of these steps and take care to support the developing professional person to ensure that he reaches his marketing potential.

The manager should be mindful of the two different areas where the marketing-oriented person may need help: signs of emotional frustration, and motivating the person in a (professional) sales environment. Some managers are inclined to think that these activities are largely a waste of time. Such managers, who frequently score high on the entrepreneurial and or aggressive trait, think that professional personnel who can sell are born and not made and that little can be done to modify the genetic code and behavior pattern, once established. This so-called nature-nurture issue has been debated for as long as psychology has been considered scientific, and it is still a contested topic. It appears that some people do possess a natural predisposition to successfully market professional services better than others, but almost everyone can improve their sales ability (or any other ability) with training, coaching, and informed feedback.

In most organizations, a relatively small number of the personnel are responsible for a majority of the selling activity. Just because this pattern exists does not mean that it is set in stone. In fact, it suggests that if the people who do little selling could concentrate on this activity a small portion of the time, overall sales revenue could climb significantly. Not everyone in a professional service organization should be a dominant sales person, and most professional people can learn to market themselves and their firm's products more effectively. The role of the manager in this process is critical to the overall success of the marketing effort.

Since the vast majority of professional personnel are learning to become better sales people, it is wise to focus on their concerns. These people are willing to accept the rejection that is a necessary part of the process, but they will need some emotional support while learning to deal with this aspect of the business. In time, they will learn the rules of the sales process and become both more successful and less vulnerable to the negative aspects of the job.

Strangely, some of the people who need the most help in the sales process are the least willing to accept it. They may be convinced that the manager is there to watch, monitor, and correct their behavior—without making any positive contribution. These people are quick to point out that they are professional and sought out this very career in order to avoid "close and unnecessary" supervision. Moreover, they may be convinced that the manager is not an especially good "presenter" himself and therefore can add little meaningful substance to their development. This attitude, when combined with the natural difficulty of selling—especially for the first time—is a barrier to success that can lead to frustration. Managers need to understand the indicators of this type of behavior and deal with the signs quickly. If frustration is allowed to fester, especially in a selling situation, then the difficulty of making a positive sales presentation can become even greater in the person's thinking, thus leading to greater frustration.

Overachiever. Indices of frustration for the overachiever will only show themselves under fairly intense pressure. He is not quick to complain or accept defeat of his ability to perform some function. He may admit to himself that he is not a natural at the sales process, but he will also be very slow to admit that most tasks can be reduced to some method that *can* be learned, and that he is determined to learn the method of sales. So when the overachiever complains or shows signs of frustration, it is because he is near a potential burn-out time. This can be evidenced by actual physical sickness, possibly near exhaustion. He is disinclined to admit defeat to any cause and will redouble his efforts to accomplish his assigned goals, but with some difficulty.

The best advice for him at this point may simply be to take some time off from the activity and return with a fresh perspective. He will grudgingly take the time off but will generally return with renewed enthusiasm. Once he does return (and presumably he is reasonably refreshed), the over-achiever needs to be politely encouraged to return to the task and rededi-cate himself to it. When dealing with the true overachiever, this form of gentle nudge is sufficient to motivate him to focus on the task at hand. However, praise can be added for the progress he has shown, and he can be subtly informed of the respect he has gained from his peers for the progress he has shown. In general, occasional, but not overly obvious, forms of positive reinforcement for his efforts and achievement will go a long way in inspiring him to continue and finish his work.

Entrepreneur. In direct contrast to the overachiever, the entrepreneur shows his frustrations more readily. He will typically focus on a discussion of money "to be made" in the future. Remember, he considers himself something of a natural marketing person (he prefers the title of marketer to sales person) and assumes that it is only a matter of time before the "fish begin to bite." He is already a firm believer in himself and his abilities, but his behavior can become increasingly self-centered and self-indulgent. He may make light of other people's accomplishments and seek attention for himself in a playful and almost childlike manner. He is not above throwing tantrums in order to get attention.

His production may decrease, and he will delegate increasing amounts of his legitimate work to subordinates and associates. He will maintain that "his" time is too important and that he needs to concentrate on his sales activity. His real motivation is simply increased levels of attention from people in positions of authority. He will see himself as entitled to preferential treatment and may demand that he receive it. He will imply that a "big sale" is right around the corner and that he needs a small advance or some other favor in order to bring it off. Finally, since he is inclined to gamble on himself, he may show signs of foolish risk taking and sports betting. He will comment that his luck is bound to turn around and that his "ship is sure to come in soon."

The obvious inappropriateness of this behavior needs to be pointed out to him quickly and firmly. He needs to understand that he will receive no special "slack, favors, cash advances, or loans" until his luck improves. He needs to be reminded that he has chosen his career path and needs to discipline himself to make it happen through his own efforts. These measures may seem formal and harsh, but the problem is that if he is successful in selling his manager on his need for special attention, then he will return to this form of behavior whenever he is tired of the sales process. Even if this prescribed managerial behavior sounds harsh, it is the one lesson that he understands best, and it will enable him to return to his most effective self the quickest.

Once he does turn the corner and begin the best use of his natural talents, he can be praised for his continued good work. Generally, these compliments should focus on his sense of pragmatism and ingenuity in completing a "difficult" assignment. The entrepreneur sees every assignment as fairly easy but thoroughly enjoys hearing others describe his accomplishment of a difficult task. Flattery is a great form of motivation for him. He is enticed with the thought that others may be slightly jealous of him. This perception is based on his own real jealousy of others. Like many people, he assumes that the factors that motivate him, motivate everyone. He is eager to win plaques, awards, and trophies. Hence, commenting on his recently acquired physical possessions will suggest to him that you recognize his superior achievements. This is flattering to him, and he will be inspired to acquire even more indices of business success.

Active. The highly active person is not easily discouraged and rarely has a "bad day." However, it does happen. The active person operates on physical/emotional energy. When this source of energy runs low, he can begin to show signs of frustration, wear, and downheartedness. It does not readily happen with the person who is primarily active, and so it is all the more noticeable when it does occur. The first telltale sign may be that he has even more difficulty concentrating on details and operating in a systematic fashion. The active is known more for his high level of energy than his focused drive, but he will customarily show some interest in detail and task completion. When he constantly seeks new activity and does not complete his current tasks, and when he fights doing any detailed analysis of a task, then he is showing signs of deep frustration.

The active person is also known as a team-oriented, group-focused person who delights in contributing to a common goal. He lives by the standard of, "One for all, and all for one." When this sense of collegial interest breaks down and he seemingly would rather fight than talk, he is frustrated about something. The source may be personal or directly work related, but it will limit his effectiveness at work. The active is known as a well-meaning person, and if he becomes socially negative and partially biting in his comments, then his behavior can have a negative effect on the entire group. He is generally seen as the person anyone can turn to for a positive comment or an encouraging word. If this does not happen, he is frustrated.

He is hitting a low point if he openly shows sadness or significant degrees of caution in his work. He is, by definition, optimistic, so even a neutral stance is a suggestion of a problem for him. However, outright moodiness is a real indication of an underlying concern. He may also show signs of increased giddiness, or almost frantic sociability and desire for meaningless social interaction. He may be eager to return to happier times when he was the genuine life of the party, and he may try to hide his real feelings of anxiety in a masquerade of comically presented humor.

The active may not initially realize that he is in a down mood, but in time he will come to accept that his behavior is different from his normal pattern. This self-awareness is the first step in bringing him out of his emotional slide and back to his productive self. Typically, it happens when a friend or business associate candidly asks him, "John, what's wrong with you? You don't seem to be your normal, upbeat self." This simple recognition by another person can start the return of the more traditional active behavior pattern. This positive trend can be continued by emphasizing the positive and contagious effect his goodwill has on other team members.

Remind him of how much better the group seems to work when he is "on." Let him know that you and the group members appreciate his flexibility, implied leadership, and ability to take a task and run with it. It is important to project a positive attitude yourself when working to modify the active's behavior. He will sense your positive vibrations and respond to them as much as the words you say. He is a person who is influenced by his environment, and although he likes to be the catalyst who starts the emotional excitement, he is affected by the general morale of the people around him.

Active-passive. In the normal course of events, the person represented by the passive trait would be discussed here. However, the primarily passive person is rare in professional services and so we will concentrate on a more typical pattern that includes a heavy portion of the passive behavior pattern. This trait pattern is represented by the person who demonstrates the active-passive behavior style. The active-passive person shows real interest in human relations. He demonstrates concern for those he meets casually and he is polite to all: fellow consultants, company presidents, waitresses, and cab drivers alike. He talks of his family with respect and feeling, and shows concern for the family of business associates.

This considerate person is generally secure in his ability and confident in his skills, as long as he is progressing in his career in a reasonably orderly manner. He does not indulge in behavior that is calculated to impress. He is just a regular and very likeable person. However, like most likeable people, he will experience his share of frustrations, and when this happens he needs some emotional support to lift him out of the doldrums.

One of the most common signs of his discomfort will be an appreciable rise in his anxiety level. He can become sick to his stomach or otherwise physically upset at seemingly normal occurrences. A random event that under most circumstances would not upset him may send him into a tailspin of worry, cause an anxiety attack, or generally ruin his day. Deadlines, real or imagined, imposed by clients or internally decreed, will cause him to lose his self-control and lash out at someone. He will seem angry and increasingly pessimistic and moody. He may become caustic to the point that people avoid contact with him.

His normally balanced sense of self-deprecating humor will be turned on others, and he can become harping and even malicious in describing others' minor foibles. Finally, he may sulk and bemoan the "good old days" when the operation was somehow different. This behavior pattern, if not corrected soon, will continue for some time. However, if noticed and called to his attention, he may have one final outburst and then return to his more normal, occasionally self-doubting, but generally optimistic self.

In order to help him out of his state, start by commenting positively on something small that he accomplished well. As a rule, he will be grateful for the attention and thoughtfulness. Mention to him that you count on his dependability, consistency, and ability to work with little supervision. Suggest that you need him back in the game, taking a leadership position, and helping others define their contribution. He is typically *not* a formal leader, but he can be a solid source of group comfort and reassurance, and in that sense he is a second-in-command type leader. Once he begins to show positive signs, encourage him to keep up the good work and suggest that others have recently commented on his new and positive demeanor. Let him know that you appreciate his ability to roll with the punches and that you are glad to see him back to his former self.

Sensitized. The professional person who demonstrates a high degree of the sensitized trait is not frequently on the front line of sales activity. However, he frequently is a technical specialist who is used in conjunction with a more sociable professional, and so he can play an important role in the overall sales process. He is generally somewhat shy, and his behavior reflects his interest in *things* rather than people. He is occasionally socially ill at ease, which is part of his normal repertoire of behavior. However, when he is frustrated these typical behavior patterns will become even more pronounced. He will appear overly shy and withdrawn. He may openly prefer to avoid contact with people and even slip into periods of daydreaming. Although this apparent dreaming may happen when he is being productive also, the difference is that when productive, these periods will result in a burst of creative energy that can lead to some form of technical breakthrough and significant increase in overall productivity. Conversely, when he is frustrated he can mentally escape and begin meandering discussions about the latest science fiction story he is reading. Further evidence of his frustration is that he will refuse work loads that normally would interest him. He will engage in meaningless conversations about increasingly trivial topics. It may appear impossible to talk directly about basic work projects to him. In essence, his mind and head will be in the clouds.

He will need a serious but subtle discussion. Once his attention is focused on the issues at hand, he can best be complimented on a job he has performed well. He will understand and accept the implied credit for himself. He will appreciate the fact that you were sufficiently perceptive to recognize his work directly and personally. Remember, he is shy and prefers to avoid the direct spotlight. A letter of commendation addressed to him with a copy to his personnel file will serve this same purpose. Open flattery, especially in front of others, should be avoided. It may, in fact, backfire and cause him increased distress. Let him know in indirect ways that you appreciate his contribution, especially in the creative and technical areas where he is probably the most comfortable.

Aggressive. The person typified by the aggressive behavior style is not easily discouraged from accomplishing his goals. As the name implies, he is a "take charge" sort of person and seldom stops until he has reached his objective. However, even these people face difficulties that can temporarily seem insurmountable. At these times, the aggressive person will show signs of frustration and negativity, which include being overly sensitive and concerned with even the slightest abuse or perceived threat to his status or position in the organization. The immaterial source of these threats is inconsequential to the "sensed" reality of their existence. The aggressive person becomes increasingly sensitive to anyone who may be a possible threat to his position or power.

He can increasingly blame others or the infamous "them" for the failure of his ideas, products, or sales presentations. Their actual culpability may be impossible to explain, but the aggressive will be sure that they are out to ruin him. Moreover, according to him, the very fact of his recent failures is proof that "they" are having some initial success. If this process continues, he can become openly belligerent and increasingly verbal, domineering, and even authoritative with peers. Finally, he can create a cause to rally his peers *against* the policies and procedures of the company. In this instance, his imagination has gone too far, and he will need a serious and candid discussion about the factual issues of his performance.

When bringing him around to the proper perspective on his success, tell him candidly that you admire his sense of determination and achievement drive. He admires these traits in himself and will be grateful that someone also sees them. Suggest that he is one of the cornerstones of the business (unit, division, company) and that his level-headed and persevering ways are needed to maintain the forward penetration in the marketplace. Openly and publicly applaud his achievements—he loves an appreciative audience—and show how he compares favorably to others.

This approach is only useful, of course, when it is valid. Give him fact-based flattery and respect for his achievements. However, be sure the data is solid because he is generally suspicious of supplicants who simply laud his behavior. In the end, bring him around gently but firmly to understand his own motivations and more effectively use them to determine his future in the organization. He will listen to sound advice that is focused on his well-being.

Compulsive. The person typified by a high degree of the compulsive trait is uncommon in society in general, although more frequently he is found in professional service firms than elsewhere. His methodical, and detailed preparation for presentations can be legendary, and hence his presence is usually quite noticeable. Even this person will show signs of frustration at some point in his career. Typical signs include an emotional overreaction to comparatively small incidents in the office. This is especially noticeable because the highly compulsive person is frequently unemotional in his reactions to most office behavior.

Alternatively, another sign of frustration may be an increase in his already highly focused attention to detail and methodical work processes. This concentration on detail per se can cause him to lose sight of the larger picture, and he will become more concerned with tactics than with the overall strategy of the marketing plan. In some ways, he develops tunnel vision and can only see the most immediate impact of his actions and plans. At these times, he needs to take a quick step back and allow his vision to expand so that he can see the larger plan.

It is generally *not* wise to interrupt him in the middle of a task to praise him, but once he does take a brief respite, slip in some economical and direct words of encouragement. Although he operates in a seeming state of mechanical efficiency, he is impressed with those who take the time to understand his projects and who comment on some specific portion of his work. The comment should be carefully measured to show an understanding of the process or project for unfocused, even well-intentioned, comments can backfire with him. One particular area that can be mentioned is his overall clear-headed and logical thinking. This is almost always true of him, so it should probably be spiced with some flavor for a specific part of his current task.

Professional service firm executives should consider all available evidence when assessing managerial potential. Performance appraisals, personnel inventories, career path plans, psychological evaluations, and job histories provide evidence but cannot replace subtle observation and insight. Many cues must be evaluated. When most evidence is favorable, the consultant may become a solid manager.

Chapter Nine

SUMMARY AND CONCLUSIONS

Including the words *personality, marketing*, and *professional services* in the title of one book may seem like either a non sequitur or a contradiction in terms to some people. It is neither, and is, in fact, quite intentional. The personalities and behavior styles of marketing/sales personnel have been extensively studied and documented. Professional people who perform a sales function have long been thought of as professional individuals who just happen to perform a marketing/sales function. Members of this school of thought suggest that these personnel and the marketing or sales functions they perform can be easily performed by anyone, that professional people who "happen" to market services are no different from those who do not market them. They are thought to just announce their availability and perform a professional service as the need arises.

This text is informed by an alternative viewpoint. It is the premise of this book that such assumptions are either naive or uninformed. Marketing and sales are critical functions of any professional service firm, and the people who can perform them best will be appropriately rewarded. It is important to recognize the fact that professional services are proactively marketed and sold, and that some people are better equipped to perform this function than others. This book is about identifying those types of people whose personalities (behavior styles) are more likely to prove successful in the marketing of professional services.

Marketing and sales are processes that begin and end with people. Somebody sells something to someone. Accordingly, this book focuses on people and the behavior styles they demonstrate in dealing with life. This understanding of personal styles is basic to appreciating everything else that follows in the text.

Some individuals will eagerly say that all people are different, that everyone has his or her idiosyncrasies that identify them as separate, unique individuals. However, some of these same people will also blandly comment that "sales" people are all the same. They are in some combination generally outgoing, usually money motivated, and prone to being socially aggressive. Other people will tell you that sales people are as different as snowflakes. Understanding people, or more appropriately, accepting that people are both unique and typical is at the core of this book. This leads to the conclusion that the many professional firms must *identify the qualified individuals with raw talent* and develop those individuals into a professional service-marketing force. This is not an easy task. Oftentimes, very capable marketing-oriented professional people can be loosely categorized into one of four categories:

Type 1. Technically capable, but honestly ignorant. They are the least experienced in marketing, and they may have little insight into the interpersonal skills required to be effective in a marketing-oriented professional firm. Consequently, they act with a high amount of genuine honesty about themselves. They will mention a desire to work with state-of-the-art technology, or an interest in working with socially responsible clients. Alternatively, they may inquire about the possibility of earning a bonus, or how long it takes to become a partner. The key to these types of people (whatever their overall behavior style) is their complete and almost naive sense of honesty. They may be highly capable, but they need time or an appropriate interviewing platform to explain their marketing potential.

Type 2. The second group, also typically with little or no real marketing experience, "think" that they have analyzed the situation very carefully and are clearly prepared for whatever questions they can be asked. In brief, these people are so anxious to strut their stuff that their transparent level of skill is easily discerned. Some of these people may actually possess the potential to develop the marketing-oriented skills necessary to qualify for the position, although this will require some time and development. In this case, the interviewer is required to see beyond the veneer that they present and read the real person.

Type 3. The third group is represented by the person whose record and appearance suggest a solid degree of discipline, achievement, motivation, emotional energy, and polite social aggressiveness. In other words, this person, presuming he possesses the education and technical skills, seems to have the overall interpersonal skills to be effective in marketing professional services. He readily shows a high degree of self-confidence, is socially engaging, and interacts well with others. He can subtly dominate a conversation but also know how to draw out other less verbal members of the group. In essence, he is a leader and it shows.

Type 4. Members of the fourth group are fairly rare. In this instance the candidates are somewhat shy and socially introverted. However, a review of their entire history suggests that they possess the discipline and ability to mature into the position and become truly exceptional professionals. In this case again, the interviewer must see beyond the immediate presentation package of the person and analyze the person who is waiting to be developed in the right environment.

As this brief review suggests, many skills and traits are combined to form the potentially successful marketing-oriented professional. The use of scientific selection procedures will generally increase the probability that fully qualified individuals are selected, trained, developed, and retained by the firm. This process begins with the use of valid employee selection instruments. Such instruments can improve the quality of the professional personnel who enter the organization by identifying those candidates who are likely to be successful *and* unsuccessful in any given position in the organization. It is well established that such an identification process can save the company money and administrative difficulties.

The generally accepted set of rules needed to establish the validity of any selection instruments are contained in the American Psychological Association's *Standards for Educational and Psychological Testing.*[1] However, the particular steps necessary to construct a valid selection instrument can vary according to the particular circumstances of the situation. For that reason, some companies have chosen to work with outside consultants to ensure the validity of their selection instruments. These assignments can vary from the consultant who completes all of the work necessary to produce a valid set of selection instruments to the consultant who can supervise and occasionally spot-check the development of the instruments by the company.

Some areas of the assignment are more efficiently completed by individuals in the personnel department, and others are more ably completed by outside professionals. In any case, joint work is generally more effective because the results are more readily accepted and can show greater scientific validity. Therefore, the results are more predictive in the selection process. In such situations, the final authority for following procedures rests with the consultant, but the ultimate responsibility for the overall validity of the process is shared by both the consultant and the firm. An abbreviated list of the steps necessary to complete the process follows.

Step 1. Review the firm's existing material and the conclusions drawn to define: (a) the job analysis, (b) the job descriptions, (c) the job specification, and (d) the job classification to determine the skill, ability, knowledge, and aptitude necessary to perform each job. In other words, create a SKAP profile for the position.

This step frequently has been completed already, and it is generally the expectation that the basic steps were completed quite accurately. It is assumed that the jobs can be meaningfully combined into a number of job families. Many of the positions possess overlapping duties and can be generally defined using more inclusive criteria. In this case, the number of jobs can be reduced from the six marketing levels to a lesser number. Realistically, some overlap exists among the six levels.

Step 2. Determine the value of either (a) using generic off-the-shelf instruments to measure the traits that are key to each of the job families defined above, or (b) develop custom instruments to measure the specific traits necessary to perform each job competently. Generally, generic tests will suffice for this purpose. However, it is impossible to determine this without completing the third step.

Step 3. Select a pilot group of employees (randomly select personnel within one of the two subgroups defined below) to complete either the generic or custom instruments. These employees will be designated by their supervisors as belonging to one of two groups: (a) very well qualified for the position, or (b) marginally qualified for the position. It is the expectation that these two groups of individuals will score differently on the instruments used to measure their skill, ability, knowledge, and aptitude to function in their given positions.

Step 4. Develop norms and comparative standards to use in the selection of future professional personnel in the company. It is frequently found that the data will reveal (using a multiple regression formula) a series of traits that are associated with success or failure in the position.

Step 5. Define and use the selection criteria to assess future employees. The long-term validity of these instruments will be measured over time, as the scores derived from the selection instruments are compared with ratings assigned to the individuals by their supervisors. It is expected that the scores of the instruments will correlate highly with the supervisor ratings. However, it is possible (and probable) that some form of modification will have to be completed after the first year.

The use of these five steps to select marketing-oriented professional service personnel requires a brief review. The first step in establishing a SKAP profile is to define the marketing skill requirements for the different positions that are being filled, that is, define the levels of marketing responsibility in the firm. Each of these levels, starting with 1 as the lowest and 6 as the highest, may be considered a step up from the previous one.

Generally speaking, the higher the number, the greater the marketing responsibilities involved. Correspondingly, the higher the number, the greater the SKAP requirements to be successful in the position.

The SKAP profile for a marketing position is the same six-step progression introduced in Chapter 1. The six steps are repeated here:

Position Level and Individual Task Responsibility Scale

6 . . . . General Management
5 . . . . Market New Products to New Clients
4 . . . . Market Existing Products to New Clients
3 . . . . Market New Products to Existing Clients
2 . . . . Market Existing Products to Existing Clients
1 . . . . Technical Competence

The task description for a marketing-oriented professional person takes on a variety of meanings. However, each of these potential meanings has its roots in a SKAP profile of the position. The definition and importance of a SKAP profile was presented in Chapter 2. The focus here is on the personal characteristics portion of the SKAP profile, as it relates to defining the behavior profile (interpersonal skills) necessary to be effective in a professional organization.

Ideally, each marketing-oriented position in the firm has its own behavior profile. This means that a candidate can be compared to a particular set of behavioral requirements for the position. Generally speaking, the higher the level of marketing responsibilities for the position in the firm, the more inclusive are the behavior profile requirements. For example, the position of vice president of sales would probably have broader requirements than the position of technical consultant. The exact behavior requirements that separate such positions are generally understood by individuals who evaluate candidates, but they are seldom explicitly stated. Such casual descriptions (or implied understandings) as "the vice president of sales has to bring in business" or "the technical consultant has to service existing accounts" are frequently heard in such descriptions.

But such well-intentioned phrases can be misleading—especially when recommendations for promotion and bonuses are being finalized. In order to correct this situation, the exact duties of the two positions (and other intervening positions) should be clarified and detailed to the greatest extent possible. The clarification of the duties (via a behavior profile) of each position will lead to improved hiring and development of professional personnel. The more professionals understand their duties, including *sales* responsibilities, the better prepared they are to deal with the consequences of their actions.

The variables necessary for each position mentioned are listed below:

1. *Knowledge*. The candidate's level of knowledge is determined by a review of such areas as education, licensing, and technical competence. Factors like education and licensing can be measured objectively. Technical competence can be evaluated during an interview by one or more of the firm's "experts." (Chapter 2)

2. *Intelligence*. The candidate's level of intelligence is most validly determined by scores on standard measures of verbal, numerical and conceptual intelligence. Simultaneously, it can be loosely gauged in an interview with writing samples, levels of spoken vocabulary and general verbal skills. (Chapter 2)

3. *Interpersonal skills*. Understanding these skills forms the foundation of the book. (Chapter 2 and elsewhere)

Defining the interpersonal skills necessary to be effective in a professional service organization is difficult for two reasons. First, agreeing on a list of interpersonal skills can be problematic. Second, once the traits are defined in the abstract sense, agreeing on which candidates demonstrate the behaviors indicative of the defined traits is also difficult.

Again, the first issue is to define the traits that are most commonly found among successful marketing-oriented and non-marketing-oriented personnel in a professional service firm. We conducted a survey among professional service personnel and found the following list of seven traits to be consistently ranked in the top ten traits of successful personnel. Coincidentally, these traits also generally match the seven behavior traits introduced earlier.

1. *Honesty*. He abides by the highest standards of professionalism. He is honest, ethical, and professional. He is self-reliant, controlled and disciplined. He stretches himself in order to reach his own high goals and standards.

2. *Competitiveness*. The degree to which the candidate is competitive. He strives to "win" and, in part, measures himself according to how well he meets or exceeds certain objectives. He is driven, goal oriented, willing to accept a calculated risk, and is diplomatically persuasive in the consulting process.

3. *Team Commitment.* He is energetic, sociable, and obviously well meaning. He likes people, and it shows. He is proud to be part of the team and is willing to sacrifice his own short-term gains for the good of the overall group. He understands that everyone is pulling together in order to make a successful group effort.

4. *Acceptance of Criticism.* He is willing to learn from a more experienced person. He may think of himself as being effective, but he also understands and accepts that he can improve his performance. He is willing to listen to honest and constructive feedback.

5. *Interpersonal Sensitivity.* He reads and reacts to people well. He understands that the basic function of the consulting process is to serve the client. He is diplomatic and sensitive to the needs of others. He is conscientious and client centered, but also strives to build a long-term relationship.

6. *Social Aggressiveness.* He is politely, socially aggressive. He will persuade, cajole, and present the benefits of the products. He will not be easily discouraged or deterred from making a presentation. At the same time, he maintains a professional and courteous approach to all customers.

7. *Administrative Follow-up.* He is detail minded and will operate in a methodical fashion. He understands and accepts the fact that the process is *not* complete until all the paper work is finished.

Professional personnel readily agree that a candidate's level of interpersonal skill, as determined by measurements of traits like those listed above, is important to success in marketing professional services. The research reported here actually measured a group of professional personnel on similar traits and determined the scores on those traits in order to differentiate between more and less successful marketing-oriented personnel. Specifically, a person's degree of the overachiever, entrepreneur, active, passive, aggressive, sensitized, and compulsive traits served to predict a person's probable success in a marketing-oriented service firm. The definitions of these traits are repeated here for convenience:

1. *Overachiever.* Stable, controlled, diligent, constructive, self-controlled and restrained.

2. *Entrepreneur.* Money motivated, competitive, driven, ambitious, goal oriented, risk taking, clever, and perceptive.

3. *Active*. Happy, sociable, well meaning, alert, enthusiastic, team oriented, and group conscious.

4. *Passive*. Sympathetic, empathic, apprehensive, occasionally anxious, inactive, and ambivalent.

5. *Aggressive*. Determined, tenacious, power seeking, suspicious, assertive, forceful, and contentious.

6. *Sensitized*. Reserved, introverted, withdrawn, secretive, perceptive, intuitive, analytical, and creative.

7. *Compulsive*. Precise, thorough, methodical, systematic, orderly, purposeful, task oriented, practical, and logical.

These factors can be measured during the interview by reviewing other books by the author.[2] The traits are *not* considered equally important. In the research reported here, the traits contributed differently to the degree of marketing success. The overachiever trait is considered universal because it is critical to all professional personnel. However, the other traits can influence a person's selling style. A person with a high level of *any combination* of the entrepreneur, active, or aggressive traits will typically have a different selling style from the person who is high on *any combination* of the passive, sensitized, or compulsive traits.

The first set of traits—entrepreneur, active, and aggressive—is associated with behavior that is found among sales development-oriented individuals. The next set of traits—passive, sensitized, and compulsive—is less common among sales development personnel but is more common among sales service-oriented individuals. The overachiever trait is considered universal because it is found among marketing and non-marketing-oriented individuals alike.

Different combinations of these traits can be used to define a candidate's behavior style and his or her potential for success. However, it is important to recognize that the overachiever trait is the *most important trait* of the seven. The level of this trait that a person possesses will determine the amount of *control* he or she has over the remaining traits. This degree of control will affect the entire behavior profile. For example, a person with a high degree of the overachiever trait and a high degree of the entrepreneur trait will show a much different behavior pattern from a person with a low degree of the overachiever and a high amount of the entrepreneur.

The former person (high overachiever, high entrepreneur) will be controlled, driven, achievement motivated, and interested in achieving monetary goals, but he will do so with a strict adherence to company policies and the norms of society. The latter person (low overachiever, high entrepreneur) will be primarily interested in acquiring money, status, and prestige and will tend to use any available means to acquire these things. He is less concerned with abiding by social norms and more concerned with his own short-term desires and self-defined needs.

Again, it is important to note that while the four characteristics of discipline, competitive drive, emotional energy, and social aggressiveness are associated with individuals who achieve marketing success, they are *not* the only traits associated with individual success in a marketing-oriented organization. Individuals who do not necessarily show a high degree of these traits can and will be successful in a marketing-oriented professional service organization.

The additional responsibility of marketing necessitates increased interpersonal skills. The interpersonal skills needed to be successful in a professional service organization require some attention or acknowledgement. The question becomes "what additional interpersonal skills does a professional person need in order to be an effective sales person within the professional environment?"

There are many "laundry lists" of interpersonal sales or marketing skills. These lists can be reviewed, and the relevant skills can be adopted or modified to fit the specific needs of any professional service organization. The list we have found to be most effective is fairly short. It focuses on the essential behavior traits necessary to be effective in a marketing-oriented professional service organization. Again, people who do not necessarily demonstrate these particular behavior traits are not considered to be less important. They can and do have a critical role to play. However, for an organization to develop a marketing orientation to client relationships, these traits are essential for some of the people in the firm.

Once the individuals with differing behavior styles are assessed, recruited, and enlisted into the organization, they can be developed to reach their full potential. The focus of the management they receive, including their training, compensation, and supervision, needs to address their individual behavior styles. Paying attention to the professional as an individual will lead to an increase in the individual's ability to market/sell the firm's professional services.

The focus of the text really is to increase the marketing/sales efforts of the firm per se. Marketing/sales is a developmental process composed of many changing parts. Marketing-oriented professional personnel, like most people, possess a certain behavior style that is formed when the person reaches legal adulthood. A person's behavior pattern exists, and some of these people develop into sales personnel. The manner or strategy a person uses to sell a given product generally evolves over time and experience. Companies may intend to adopt a specific strategy to market a product, but the actual operating strategy probably will develop over time. This sales strategy is influenced by sales training programs, compensation packages, and the managerial hierarchy of the firm, but the strategy that proves most effective is a direct outgrowth of the behavior style of the professional people who are doing the selling.

The structure of a sales force can be pre-ordained in someone's mind, but the pragmatic structure that results generally requires time to grow and develop a certain definition of its own. This structure is an outgrowth of the people who make up the company. Likewise, any system used to monitor and measure success in a sales activity can be defined at the conception of the product, but often it is modified over time by the people in the organization. Finally, understanding the marketing-oriented people who compose the professional services organization is the key to understanding the organization as a whole.

NOTES

1. American Psychological Association, *Standards for Educational and Psychological Testing* (Washington, D.C.: APA, 1985).

2. James B. Weitzul, *Evaluating Interpersonal Skills in the Job Interview: A Guide for Human Resource Professionals* (Westport, Conn.: Quorum Books, 1992); and James B. Weitzul, *Sales Force Dynamics: Motives, Management, Money, Marketplace* (Westport, Conn.: Quorum Books, 1993).

SELECTED BIBLIOGRAPHY

Aronson, E. *The Social Animal.* 3d ed. San Francisco: W. H. Freeman & Co., 1980.

Barnard, C. *The Functions of the Executive.* Cambridge: Harvard University Press, 1938.

Bass, B. M., and P. C. Burger. *Assessment of Managers: An International Comparison.* New York: Free Press, 1979.

Bennis, W. J., Van Maanen, and E. H. Schein, eds. *Essays in Interpersonal Relations.* Homewood, Ill.: Dorsey Press, 1979.

Brazerman, M. H., and R. J. Lewicki, eds. *Negotiation in Organizations.* Beverly Hills: Sage Publications, 1983.

Crissy, W.J.E., W. H. Cunningham, and I.C.M. Cunningham. *Selling: The Personal Force in Marketing.* New York: John Wiley & Sons, 1977.

Cyert, R. M., and J. G. March. *A Behavioral Theory of the Firm.* Englewood Cliffs, N.J.: Prentice-Hall, 1963.

Darmon, Rene Y. *Effective Human Resource Management in the Sales Force.* Westport, Conn.: Quorum Books, 1992.

Drucker, P. *The Practice of Management.* New York: Harper, 1954.

Festinger, L. *A Theory of Cognitive Dissonance.* Evanston, Ill.: Row Peterson, 1957.

Forsyth, D. E. *An Introduction to Group Dy amics.* Monterey, Calif.: Brooks/Cole Publishing, 1983.

Hall, C. S., and G. Lindzey. *Theories of Personality.* 3d ed. New York: John Wiley & Sons, 1978.

Kotler, P. *Marketing Management.* 3d ed. Englewood Cliffs, N.J.: Prentice-Hall, 1976.

Kotter, J. P. *The General Managers.* New York: Free Press, 1982.

——— . *Power and Influence: Beyond Formal Authority.* New York: Free Press, 1985.

Lawler, E. E. *Pay and Organizational Development*. Reading, Mass.: Addison-Wesley, 1981.

McClelland, D. C. *Human Motivation*. Glenview, Ill.: Scott Foresman, 1985.

Odiorne, G. S. *Management and the Activity Trap*. New York: Harper & Row, 1974.

Peters, T. *Liberation Management*. New York: Knopf, 1992.

Peterson, R. *Personal Selling*. New York: John Wiley & Sons, 1978.

Russel, F. A., F. H. Beach, and F. H. Buskirk. *Textbook of Salesmanship*. 10th ed. New York: McGraw-Hill, 1978.

Stanton, W. J., and R. J. Buskirk. *Management of the Sales Force*. 4th ed. Homewood, Ill.: Richard D. Irwin, 1974.

Townsend, R. *Up the Organization*. New York: Knopf, 1970.

Vroom, V. H., and P. W. Yetton. *Leadership and Decision Making*. Pittsburgh: University of Pittsburgh Press, 1973.

Webster, F. E., Jr. *Industrial Marketing Strategy*. New York: John Wiley & Sons, 1979.

Weitzul, James B. *Evaluating Interpersonal Skills in the Job Interview: A Guide for Human Resource Professionals*. Westport, Conn.: Quorum Books, 1992.

———. *Sales Force Dynamics: Motives, Management, Money, Marketplace*. Westport, Conn.: Quorum Books, 1993.

INDEX

American Psychological Association, 149

appraisal. *See* performance appraisal

assessment: active candidate and, 52–54; adaptability and, 49; aggressive candidate and, 56–57; compulsive candidate and, 57–58; drive and, 48; entrepreneur candidate and, 51–52; interview topics and, 47–49; overachiever candidate and, 49–51, 58–59; passive candidate and, 54–55; risk-taking and, 48; self-esteem and, 47–48; sensitized candidate and, 55–56; stress tolerance and, 48–49; trait combinations and, 59–61; trait indicators and, 45–47

behavior profile, 151–52, 154–55

behavior traits/styles: appraisal systems and, 106; constancy of, 36; development and service orientation and, 154; interpersonal skills and, 26–27; list compilation and, 30–31; listed and defined, 29–30, 153–54; overachiever and, 29, 30–31, 36, 94, 108, 154; performance appraisal and, 108–9; recruitment process and, 31–32, 45 (*see also under* assessment; enlistment); of sales manager, 92–93, 100 (*see also under* leadership); sales presentation style and, 99–100; of sales trainee, 93–95 (*see also under* leadership); selling style and, 154; study on, 31–37; success factor and, 29, 31–32, 34, 36, 37, 147, 154–56. *See also under* compensation; performance appraisal; training

compensation: active trait and, 121, 124; active-passive trait and, 122; aggressive trait and, 119, 120, 121, 122, 124; compulsive trait and, 125; defined, 105; entrepreneur trait and, 119–20, 121, 122, 123–24; forms of, 105; importance of, 119–20; overachiever trait and, 119, 123; passive trait and, 121, 124; recruitment and, 120–21; retention and, 123–25; reward and, 121–23; sensitized trait and, 124–25

About the Author

JAMES B. WEITZUL is President of Banks & Weitzul, a Princeton, N.J., consulting firm. He is the author of two previous Quorum books, *Evaluating Interpersonal Skills in the Job Interview: A Guide for Human Resource Professionals* (1992) and *Sales Force Dynamics: Motives, Management, Money, Marketplace* (1993).

DATE DUE